華 文 讀 本

第 二 冊

READ CHINESE

Book II

by Richard F. Chang

張 一 峰

FAR EASTERN PUBLICATIONS
YALE UNIVERSITY
NEW HAVEN, CONNECTICUT

ISBN 0-88710-066-X

INTRODUCTION TO READ CHINESE, Book Two

READ CHINESE, Book One, the first volume in
the MIRROR SERIES (for reading) introduces the student
to three hundred basic Chinese characters. This book,
READ CHINESE, Book Two, presents an additional three
hundred. The third volume in the series (READ CHINESE,
Book Three) introduces four hundred, making a total
of one thousand basic characters. Students who use
this series should be thoroughly familiar with the
basic spoken patterns of the language as they are introduced in SPEAK CHINESE (beginning text) and CHINESE
DIALOGUES (intermediate level text) or other comparable
texts.

This text comprises fifteen lessons, each of
which presents twenty new characters. The new characters
are for the most part, selected from the frequency list
issued by the People's Republic of China, so the student
can be sure that all the characters and the various combinations are worth learning for the future. Each lesson contains, in addition to the new character display
pages, a story (GÙSHR/gùshi), a list of sentences for
additional practice (JYÙDZ/jùzi), and the new vocabulary
list. No new combinations or sentence patterns are introduced, except those which the student has learned
already from either SPEAK CHINESE or CHINESE DIALOGUES.
In fact, the content of the stories, the subject matter
and the expressions used, are closely related to the
contents of CHINESE DIALOGUES.

The Sentences are meant to provide additional
practice and review. After a new character is used in
the Story, it also appears four or more times in the
Sentences of that lesson, and it appears again in the
Sentences in every two or three lessons thereafter.
In the expanded edition published in 1983 the Sentences
are also printed in simplified characters in order to
provide practice in this form of the Chinese character.

The New Character Display pages present each of the twenty new characters in their traditional, complex form. If a character has a simplified form, it is printed in the lower right hand corner of the square. Each new character is defined in English and also defined grammatically. In addition these pages present common terms and expressions for immediate practice within the context of the new character. Each word and each expression is pronounced in both Yale and Pinyin (mainland) romanization. It is hoped that by providing both romanization systems, this book can achieve wider use. Students are urged to learn at least one romanization system thoroughly. However, at the present time, there are at least three romanization system in common use: the Yale System, the Pinyin System and the Wade-Giles System. The Yale system is used primarily in teaching texts published by Yale University but it is also used in many of the teaching programs on Taiwan. The Pinyin System is, of course, the officially approved system in use in China while the Wade-Giles System is used in English language books on China. The latter system in also still used in library card files.

The Vocabulary List for each lesson includes the new words (pronounced and defined) and also shows the meaning of the individual character once again for reinforcement. It is an excellent idea for students to learn the meaning of the individual character as well as the combination because the individual character will reappear later in combinations not included in this book.

Since its publication this book has been widely used by many colleges, many of whom do not utilize the companion text, CHINESE DIALOGUES. Therefore, some time back, a more comprehensive vocabulary list was prepared which did not assume prior use of CHINESE

DIALOGUES, but <u>does</u> assume prior mastery of SPEAK CHINESE and READ CHINESE, Book One (vocabulary and patterns).

For the benefit of those students who use this text and CHINESE DIALOGUES at the same time, the author has prepared the following chart to show the relationship between the vocabularies of the two books:

READ CHINESE, Book Two		CHINESE DIALOGUES
Lesson 1	*corresponds to Lesson*	*1-5*
2		*1-6*
3		*1-7*
4		*1-7*
5		*1-8*
6		*1-12*
7		*1-15*
8		*1-16*
9		*1-17*
10		*1-18*
11		*1-19*
12		*1-20*
13		*1-21*
14		*1-24*
15		*1-24*

As the reader will see shortly, in addition to the parts of speech used in SPEAK CHINESE and READ CHINESE, Book One, this book also uses the following: FV for Functive Verb (that is, a verb that can take an object); PH for Phrase; PAT for pattern and AT for attributive.

The author wishes to express his gratitude to all the friends and colleagues who have helped him in the preparation of this book.

R. F. Chang

TABLE OF CONTENTS

LESSON 1

Characters	Explanations	Expressions
夏	*SYÀ* *xià* BF: *summer*	夏天 TW: summer
預 预	*YÙ* BF: *beforehand*	預先 A: beforehand 預(先)定 V: decide before-hand; order or subscribe for (as a new book about to be published) 預備 V: prepare
備 备	*BÈI* BF: *prepare*	預備 V: prepare
海	*HǍI* N: *sea*	上海 PW: Shanghai 海魚 N: salt water fish 海邊兒 N: seashore
姐	*JYĚ* *jiě* BF: *older sister, young lady*	姐姐 jyějye N: older sister 小姐 syáujye N: Miss; polite for some one else's daughter

1

Characters	Explanations	Expressions	
介	JYÈ jiè	介紹	V: introduce, recommend
紹 绍	SHÀU shào	介紹 介紹信	V: introduce, recommend N: a letter of introduction
冬	DŪNG dōng	冬天	TW: winter
畢 毕	BÌ	畢業	VO: graduate
業 业	YÈ	畢業 工業	VO: graduate N: industry

Characters	Explanations	Expressions
接	*JYĒ* *jiē* V: receive, meet (at a train, boat, etc.); connect with	接着 jyējáu RV: received, met 接朋友 VO: meet and escort friend
封	*FĒNG* M: (for letters)	信封儿 N: envelope 一封信 N: a letter
里	*LǏ* M: a Chinese li (about 1/3 mile)	一里路 N: one li 海里 N: nautical mile
鄉 乡	*SYĀNG* *xiāng* BF: the country (as contrasted with the town)	鄉下 PW: the country, rural district 下鄉 VO: go to the country
秋	*CHYŌU* *qiū* BF: autumn	秋天 TW: autumn

Characters	Explanations	Expressions
談 谈	*TÁN*　　V: chat, talk about	談一談　V: chat for awhile 談話　　VO: carry on conversation
剛 刚	*GĀNG*　A: just this minute	剛才　　MA: just a moment ago
概	*GÀI*　　BF: in general	大概　　MA: probably
共	*GÙNG*　BF: altogether *gòng*	一共　　MA: altogether, in all
春	*CHWŪN* BF: spring (season) *chūn*	春天　　TW: springtime

第一 kè　　 gù 事

　　王國平是上海人。他家在上海南邊兒的一個鄉
下，離城大概有十里路。王家一共有五個人：父親，
母親，哥哥，姐姐，跟國平。因為國平是家裏最小
的一個，所以大家都叫他小王。

　　小王的父親，王先生，是一個作買賣的。他在
上海城裏有一個鋪子。每天早上他坐火車到城裏去，
晚上天黑了才回來。中飯就在鋪子前頭的那個飯館
兒吃。王先生很會作買賣，說話也很客氣，所以鋪
子裏的買賣很不錯。

　　小王的哥哥，姐姐去年冬天在北 jīng 的北海大學
畢了業，今年春天就到美國念書去了。小王在小學
念書的時候常聽見他哥哥，姐姐說，北 jīng 那個地方
好極了。他很想跟他哥哥，姐姐一塊兒到北 jīng 去念
書。他跟他父母說了好幾次，可是他父母說他太小，
不應當出門，要他等中學畢業以後再說。

　　小王現在十六歲了，今年夏天剛念完了中學，
他很想秋天到北 jīng 去念書。有一天晚上小王跟家裏
的人吃了晚飯，就在一塊兒談話。小王對他父母說，

他想今年秋天到北jīng去念書。

王先生說:「上海有很多大學,你為甚麼一定要到北jīng去念書呢?」

小王說:「人人都說北jīng是一個好地方,我想到那兒去念書一定很有意思。」

王太太說: 北jīng離上海這麼遠,你一個人去我不放心。」

小王說:「我們學校這次有很多學生要去,我們可以一塊兒走。」

王先生說: 北jīng有很多有名的大學,到那兒去念書也不錯。我有一個老朋友姓張,他在北海大學教書。我可以預先給他寫一封信,請他到火車站去接你。你們打算哪天走?」

「我們打算下禮拜天走。」

「好,我明天就給張先生寫信。現在時候不早了,你去睡吧。」

小王看了看表說:「已經快十點鐘了!」

小王跟王先生,王太太說了明天見,就到他的屋子裏去了。

第一kè　　句 子

1.今年夏天你打算到海邊兒去麼？我有兩個姐姐都
　　打算去。

2.要是你想去我可以給你們介紹介紹。

3.我二姐是北海大學的學生，今年多天就要畢業了。

4.我剛才接着他的信，那封信上說他明天就可以到
　　上海了。

5.他打算在家裏住三四個月，再回北jīng去。

6.他這次回北jīng去大概要等畢業以後才回家。

7.我家住在鄉下離城大概三十里路。

8.要是你想到我家去你最好預先告訴我，我可以到
　　車站去接你。

9.我們鄉下有一個很好的lyú館，我可以給你預定一
　　個屋子。

10.聽說你今年秋天要到北jīng去念書，我想你最好跟
　　我二姐談談。

11.他在北jīng有很多朋友，我想他一定可以給你介紹
　　幾個。

12.你剛才說的那位王先生，他也是北海大學畢業的
　　嗎？我二姐大概認識他。

13. 我大姐現在在<u>美國</u>念書，他大概今年夏天可以回
    國。

14. 我一共有兩個姐姐，大姐姐在<u>美國</u>，二姐姐在<u>北
    jīng</u>。

15. 我剛才說的是我大姐，不是我二姐。

16. 我剛才接着大姐的信，信上說在<u>美國</u>念書眞有意
    思。

17. 聽說他的學校離海邊兒不遠。

18. 我不知道有多少里，我想大概有二三十里吧。

19. 我大姐每個禮拜給我寫一封信，上個月我一共接
    着他四封信。

20. 今年春天我接着他的一封信，信上說他今年夏天
    就可以畢業了。

21. 畢業以後他想到別的地方去玩兒。

22. 他說<u>美國</u>的鄉下很有意思，他畢業以後一定要到
    鄉下去住一個月。

23. 聽說這次畢業一共有五個<u>中國</u>學生，他們今年冬
    天回國。

24. 我已經給大姐寫了一封信，要他畢了業就回來。

25. 要是你要知道一點兒<u>美國</u>大學的事情，你可以跟

　　我大姐談談。

26.你不認識他，不要緊，我可以給你們介紹。

27.我大姐很喜歡談話，他常跟他的朋友談一天的話。

28.他常常預備了很多點心，請很多朋友到他家去吃

　　點心。

29.我大姐說，他的外國朋友都喜歡吃他預備的中國

　　點心。

30.你想給我大姐寫信嗎？我這兒有信紙信封。

Vocabulary

New characters:

海　鄉　概　里　共
姐　冬　畢　業　春
夏　剛　秋　談　預
封　接　介　紹　備

---

1. 上海　SHÀNGHĂI　PW: Shanghai (commercial
   海　HĂI　metropolis of China)
   　N: sea
2. 鄉下　SYĀNGSYA/xiāngxia PW: country, rural area
   鄉　SYĀNG/xiāng　BF: country (as contrasted
   　with town, city)
3. 大概　DÀGÀI　MA: probably
   概　GÀI　in general
4. 里　LĬ　M: (Chinese mile, about 1/3
   　English mile
5. 一共　YÍGÙNG/yígòng　MA: altogether, in all
   共　GÙNG/gòng　altogether
6. 姐姐　JYĔJYE/jiĕjie　N: older sister
   姐　JYĔ/jiĕ　older sister, young lady
7. 大家　DÀJYĀ/dàjiā　N: all, everyone
8. 冬天　DŪNGTYAN/dōngtian TW: winter
   冬　DŪNG/dōng　winter
9. 北海大學　BĔIHĂI DÀSYWÉ　N: Beihai University
   大學　— — daxúe
10. 畢業　BÌYÈ　VO: graduate

畢	BÌ		*finish, conclude*
業	YÈ		*profession, business*
11. 春天	CHWŪNTYAN/chūntian	TW:	*springtime*
春	CHWŪN/chūn		*spring (season)*
12. 小學	SYĂUSYWÉ/xiǎoxué	N:	*elementary school*
13. 中學	JŪNGSYWÉ/zhōngxué	N:	*high school, middle school*
14. 再說	DZÀISHWŌ/zàishuō	PH:	*see about it, talk further*
15. 夏天	SYÀTYAN/xiàtian	TW:	*summer (time)*
夏	SYÀ/xià		*summer*
16. 剛	GĀNG	A:	*just this minute*
17. 秋天	CHYŌUTYAN/qiūtian	TW:	*autumn*
秋	CHYŌU/qiū		*autumn*
18. 談話	TÁNHWÀ/tánhuà	VO:	*to chat, talk over*
談	TÁN		*chat, talk about*
19. 預先	YÙSYĀN/yùxiān	A:	*beforehand*
預	YÙ		*beforehand*
20. 封	FĒNG	M:	*(for letters)*
21. 接	JYĒ/jīe	FV:	*receive, meet (on arrival at train, etc.)*
22. 介紹	JYÈSHAU/jièshao	FV:	*introduce, recommend*
介	JYÈ/jiè		*lie between*
紹	SHAU/shao		*connect, join*
23. 剛才	GĀNGTSÁI/gāngcái	MA:	*just a moment ago*
24. 接着	JYĒJÁU/jīezháo	RV:	*to have met, have received*
25. 再	DZÀI/zài	A:	*then*
26. lyǔ館	LYŮGWĂN/lǘguǎn	N:	*hotel*
27. 預定	YÙDÌNG/yùdìng	FV:	*reserve, order, subscribe for*

		(as a new book about to be published)
	定	DÌNG FV: *reserve, subscribe*
28.	預備	YÙBÈI FV: *prepare for*
	備	BÈI *prepare for*
29.	信封	SYÌNFĒNG/xìnfēng N: *envelope*

LESSON 2

Characters	Explanations	Expressions
李	*LǏ* N: a surname	行李 N: baggage 姓李 surnamed Li
航	*HÁNG* BF: sail, navigage	航空 BF: aviation 航空信 N: air mail 航行 V/N: navigate/ navigation 航海 V/N: navigation (by sea)
空	*KŪNG* SV/BF: be empty, vacant/air *kōng*	航空 BF: aviation 航空信 N: air mail
熱 热	*RÈ* SV: be hot	熱心 SV: be zealous, enthusiastic 熱水 N: hot water 熱氣 N: hot air
風 风	*FĒNG* N: wind	風景 N: scenery, view, landscape

Characters	Explanations	Expressions
景	_JĬNG_ BF: scenery, view	風景 N: scenery, view, landscape
旅	_LYŬ_ BF: travel lǚ	旅館 N: hotel 旅行 V/N: travel/travel, trip
乾 干	_GĀN_ SV: be dry	乾淨 SV: be clean 乾了 SV: become dry
淨 净	_JÌNG_ BF: clean	乾淨 SV: be clean
替	_TÌ_ CV: for (in place of)	我替你去 I will go for you. 替我問他 IE: send him my 好 regards

Characters	Explanations	Expressions
間 间	*JYĀN* /M: the space between/ *jiān* (for rooms)	房間 N: room 時間 N: time, period 一間屋子 one room

特	*TÈ* BF: special(ly)	特別 SV/A: be special,
		            distinctive/
		            especially

電 电	*DYÀN* N: electricity *diàn*	電報 N: telegram, cable 電話 N: telephone 電車 N: trolley car

恐	*KǓNG* BF: afraid
	kǒng
		恐怕 V/MA: be afraid
		            that/perhaps,
		            probably

郵 邮	*YÓU* BF: postal	郵局 N: post office 郵車 N: postal vans 郵差 yóuchāi N: mail-man

Characters	Explanations	Expressions
局	*JYÚ* *jú* BF: an office, a bureau	郵局 N: post office 電報局 N: telegraph office
寄	*JÌ* V: mail, send by mail	寄信 VO: mail letters 寄東西 VO: mail things
收	*SHŌU* V: receive, collect	收到 V/RV: received, able to receive 收條ル N: a receipt 收拾 V: fix, repair, clean up, put in order, straighten out
拾	*SHŔ* *shí* V: pick up, collect/ ten (the form of 十 used in documents to prevent fraud)	收拾 V: fix, repair, clean up, put in order, straighten out
安	*ĀN* BF: peace	平安 N/SV: peace/be peaceful 一路平安 Ph: a pleasant journey

第二kè　gù 事

　　禮拜天早上剛五點鐘，小王家裏的人都已經起來了。因爲那天小王要坐早上八點鐘的火車到北jīng去，所以他家裏的人都要到火車站去送他。王先生幫着小王收拾行李。王太太特別給小王預備了很多吃的東西。王太太說：

　　「這兩天天氣熱，火車上的東西恐怕不乾淨，所以我給你預備了一點兒吃的東西。」

　　他們把行李收拾好了的時候已經七點鐘了。王先生說：

　　「時間不早了，我們走吧。我得到電報局去給張先生打一個電報。你們先到火車站去吧。」

　　王太太說：「你昨天給張先生寄了一封航空信，爲甚麼今天還要給他打電報呢？」

　　王先生說：「我恐怕航空信不够快，所以再給他打一個電報。」

　　小王跟他母親到火車站的時候，別的學生已經在那兒等着小王呢。小王把他朋友給他母親介紹了介紹。火車快開了。小王跟他的朋友都打算上車。

王先生那個時候才到火車站。

　　王先生說:「電報我已經打了。張先生大概會到
車站去接你們。」

　　王太太說:「一路平安,到了給我們寫信。」

　　小王跟他的父母說了再見就上車了。

　　過了一個禮拜,王先生,王太太接着小王寄來
的一封航空信,信上說:

　　「⋯⋯我們已經很平安的到了北jīng,路上一共走
了四天。那天張先生因為有事情,所以要他女兒替
他到火車站來接我們。張先生,張太太都很熱心,
他們特別給我收拾了一間屋子,請我在他們家住。

　　北jīng這個地方真有意思,人都很客氣,風景也
很好。這兩天不太熱,所以我們天天到風景好的地
方去玩兒。

　　剛才我跟張先生談了一會兒學校的事情。我打
算今年秋天到北海大學去念書。我很好,請你們兩
位放心。」

第二ké 句子

1. 上禮拜我接到李先生的一封航空信，信上說，他
   跟他姐姐要到這兒來旅行。

2. 他問我這兒的風景好不好。夏天熱不熱。

3. 他還問我這兒的旅館乾淨不乾淨。

4. 要是旅館乾淨，他要我替他預定一間房間。

5. 我很想見見李先生，特別想見他姐姐，所以我想
   給他們打一個電話。

6. 可是打電話恐怕很貴，所以我想最好到電報局去
   給他們打一個電報。

7. 可是我有很多話要跟李先生說，打電報恐怕也很
   貴，所以我給他們寄了一封航空信。

8. 我告訴他們說，這兒是一個鄉下地方，春天跟秋
   天時候的風景特別好。

9. 夏天不太熱，可是冬天的天氣很乾，風也很大。

10. 這兒的旅館很多，也很乾淨，可是很貴。

11. 我家有很多空屋子，我可以給你們收拾兩間，你
    們就不用住旅館了。

12. 過了幾天我又收到李先生的一封航空信。

13. 信上說，他因為有要緊的事情，恐怕不能來旅行，

所以他要他姐姐一個人來。

14.他謝謝我這麼熱心。他要我到火車站接他姐姐去。

15.李小姐一下火車就問我，我的車在哪兒，他說他
　　的行李很多。

16.我說我沒有車，我們得坐電車回去，他聽了很生
　　氣。

17.他說他有很多行李，恐怕不能坐電車。我說不要
　　緊，我可以替他拿。

18.他問我郵局在哪兒，他要去寄一封信，告訴他的
　　弟弟他已經很平安的到了。

19.我說火車站後頭的那間小屋子就是郵局。

20.李小姐說，我們這兒的郵局又小又不乾淨。

21.我們到了家，我替他把行李放在一間收拾好了的
　　屋子裏。

22.他看了看那間屋子說:「這間屋子太小，我想我到
　　旅館去住吧。」

23.我說這兒的旅館都很貴。他說貴不要緊，可是得
　　乾淨。

24.我帶他到風景好的地方去看看，他說這兒的風景
　　沒有甚麼特別。

25.我問他打算在這兒住幾天，他說他打算明天早上
　　就回去。

26.我預備了晚飯，可是他說他得收拾行李，沒有工
　　夫到我家來吃晚飯。

27.第二天早上我替他把行李送到火車站去。

28.他要我替他打一個電報，叫他弟弟到火車站去接
　　他。

29.我送他上火車，跟他說一路平安，請他有工夫再
　　到這兒來玩兒。

30.他說他不太喜歡旅行，所以恐怕不會再來了。

Vocabulary

New characters

收 拾 李 特 熱
恐 乾 淨 間 電
局 寄 航 空 安
替 風 景 旅 郵

---

1. 收拾   SHŌUSHR/shōushi   FV: *put in order, clean up*

  收   SHŌU   FV: *receive, collect*

  拾   SHŔ/shí   FV: *pick up*

2. 行李   SYÍNGLI/xíngli   N: *baggage, luggage*

  李   LǏ   N: *(surname)*

3. 特別   TÈBYÉ/tèbié   A/SV: *especially, be special, distinctive*

  特   TÈ   *special*

4. 熱   RÈ   SV: *be hot*

5. 恐怕   KǓNGPÀ/kǒngpà   MA: *perhaps, probably*

  恐   KǓNG/kǒng   *afraid*

6. 乾淨   GĀNJING   SV: *be clean*

  乾   GĀN   SV: *be dry*

  淨   JING   *clean*

7. 時間   SHŔJYĀN/shíjiān   N: *time, period*

  間   JYĀN/jiān   *space between*

8.	電報局	DYÀNBÀUJYÚ/diànbàojú	N: telegraph office
	電報	DYÀNBÀU/diànbào	N: telegram, cable
	電	DYÀN/diàn	N: electricity
	局	JYÚ/jú	office, bureau
9.	打電報	DǍ DYÀNBÀU/- diànbào	VO: send a telegram
10.	寄	JÌ	FV: mail, send by mail
11.	航空信	HÁNGKŪNGSYÌN/hángkōng- xìn	N: air mail
	航空		BF: aviation
	航	HÁNG	sail, navigate
	空	KŪNG/kōng	SV: be empty, vacant
12.	會	HWÈI/hùi	AV: may, would, could
13.	一路平安	YÍLÙPÍNGĀN	PH: have a pleasant trip
	平安	PÍNGĀN	SV: be peaceful
	安	ĀN	peace
14.	替	TÌ	CV: for (in place of)
15.	熱心	RÈSYĪN/rèxīn	SV: be enthusiastic
16.	間	JYĀN/jiàn	M: (for room
17.	風景	FĒNGJǏNG	N: scenery, landscape
	風	FĒNG	N: wind
	景	JǏNG	SCENERY
18.	旅行	LYǙSYÍNG/lǚxíng	FV/N: travel/travel, trip
	旅	LYǙ/lǚ	travel
19.	旅館	LYǙGWǍN/lǚguǎn	N: hotel
20.	空	KŪNG/kōng	SV: be vacant, empty
21.	小姐	SYǍUJYE/xiǎojie	N: Miss
22.	電車	DYÀNCHĒ/diànchē	N: street car, trolley
23.	郵局	YÓUJYÚ/yóujú	N: post office
	郵	YÓU	postal

LESSON 3

Characters	Explanations	Expressions
飛 飞	FĒI V: fly	飛機 N: airplane 起飛 V: take off
機 机	JĪ BF: opportune; machine	飛機 N: airplane 機會 N: opportunity, chance 機關 N: organization
語 语	YŬ BF: language; a set phrase	國語 N: (the Chinese) national language 日語 N: the Japanese language
午	WŬ BF: noon	上午 TW: forenoon 中午 TW: noon 下午 TW: afternoon 午飯 N: the noon meal
零	LÍNG NU: zero	一百零一 NU: one hundred and one

Characters	Explanations	Expressions
立	LÌ V: establish; stand up	立刻 A: at once 立起來 RV: stand up
票	PYÀU N: ticket piào	票房 N: ticket office 火車票 N: railroad ticket 電車票 N: trolley car ticket 飛機票 N: airplane ticket 行李票 N: baggage ticket
讓 让	RÀNG V/CV: let, allow/by (governing agent in "passive" constructions)	點心讓孩子給吃了 light refreshment has been eaten by the children
汽	CHÌ BF: steam qì	汽車 N: automobile, car
非	FĒI A: be not	非常 A: very, extraordinarily 非去不可 must go

Characters	Explanations	Expressions
希	*SYĪ* BF: hope *xī*	希望 V/N: hope
望	*WÀNG* BF: hope, expect, look at	希望 V/N: hope
記 记	*JÌ* V: remember, recollect	記得 jìde V: remember 記住 RV: fix or hold in mind
清	*CHĪNG* SV: be clear, pure, *qīng* lucid	清楚 chīngchu SV: be clear 清算 V: liquidate
楚	*CHǓ* BF: be clear, distinct	清楚 chīngchu SV: be clear

Characters	Explanations	Expressions
急	JÍ SV: be anxious, hurried, urgent, hasty	着急　jāují 　　　VO/SV: be worried, get excited 急甚麼　What's the hurry?
簡 简	JYĂN BF: be simple, concise jiǎn	簡直(的) A: simply; come to the point
停	TÍNG V: stop	停車　　VO: park a car, stop a train 停在前頭 parked in front
皮	PÍ N: bark, skin, leather, fur, peel, outer covering	皮包　　N: suitcase, brief-case, small handbag 皮子　　N: fur, leather, hide 皮子作的 Ph: made of leather
包	BĀU V/M: wrap/parcel, pack, package bāo	皮包　　N: suitcase, briefcase, small handbag 包上　　RV: wrap 包起來 RV: wrap up

第三kè　gù 事

　　有一天小王的朋友小李到張家去找小王，想跟小王談談。

　　小李說:「要是你不忙，我們到城外頭去玩兒玩兒，好不好?」

　　小王說:「這兒的鄉下我差不多都去過了，沒有甚麼意思。」

　　小李說:「我記得¹在上海的時候常聽人說天jing²是一個很大的城，跟上海一樣大。聽說那個地方非常³有意思。我們到那兒去旅行幾天，好不好?」

　　小王說:「天jing 離這兒有多少里路? 我不想到太遠的地方去。」

　　「不遠，不遠，就有一百多里路，坐飛機⁴去一個鐘頭就到了。」

　　「坐飛機太貴，我想坐火車去吧。」你知道不知道一天有幾次火車? 甚麼時候開?」

　　小李說:「這個我不太清楚⁵，可是不要緊，我立刻⁶給火車站打一個電話⁷，問一問。」

　　小王說:「你的國語⁸不太好，說不清楚，讓張小

姐替你打吧。」

「不必，不必，」小李很急的說，「我在這兒住了快兩個月了，平常的話大概都可以說。很多人說，我的國語說得簡直跟北jīng人一樣。」

小李說完了，就給火車站打電話。站上的人說：「到天jing去的火車一天兩次；上午一次，下午一次。」

「有沒有特別快車？」小李問。

「有，禮拜天早上十點零五分有一次，路上哪一站都不停，兩個鐘頭就可以到了。」

小李的國語不太好，他以爲站上的人說的是早上四點零五分。

「特別快車爲甚麼開得這麼早呢？」小王覺得不對。

小李說：「這個我也不清楚。」

禮拜天早上三點鐘小王跟小李每人拿着一個皮包從張家出來。他們坐着汽車就到火車站去了。

他們到了火車站，看見站上一個人也沒有，覺得很奇怪。

小李說：「時候不早了，恐怕人都已經上車了，

我們立刻去買票[19]吧。」

　　小李跟小王很快的跑到票房[20]那兒買了兩張票。

　　小李問賣票的說:「到天 jing 去的特別快車開了沒有?」

　　賣票的看了看他們說:「先生，你們一定 nùng 錯了[21]，特別快車上午十點零五分才開呢。」

　　小李跟小王半天沒說話。後來小李對小王說:

「這不是我的國語不好，這兒的電話簡直的聽不清楚。我希望[22]你不要跟別人說這件事。」

第三kè　　句　子

1. 請問到上海去的飛機甚麼時候起飛[23]？

2. 對不起，我的國語不好，說不清楚，我剛才說的
   是到上海去的飛機。

3. 下午四點零五分才起飛嗎？為甚麼上午沒有飛機
   起飛呢？

4. 我得立刻到票房去買票。票房的門還沒開嗎？我
   們坐下談談吧。

5. 先生，你也坐今天下午的飛機到上海去嗎？

6. 你要坐飛機到北jīng去嗎？我以為你也要到上海去。

7. 北jīng離這兒就有一百里路，你為甚麼不坐汽車去
   呢？

8. 聽說北jīng那個地方非常有意思，我希望我有機會[24]
   到那兒去旅行。

9. 我小的時候跟我姐姐去過一次，可是現在都不記
   得了。

10. 那一次是坐汽車去的，我記得我坐了一天的汽車。

11. 我記不清楚我那個時候住在甚麼地方了，大概住
    在離城不遠的一個鄉下。

12.我記得我們每天早上坐汽車到城裏去，中午就在
　　郵局前頭的那個飯館兒吃飯。

13.我記得北jīng的風景非常好，地方也很乾淨，可是
　　夏天很熱。

14.現在才三點零七分，別着急，我們還可以談一會
　　兒。

15.你的國語說得這麼好，你一定是北jīng人吧？

16.你是在北海大學畢的業嗎？我姐姐也是在北海大
　　學畢業的。

17.我不記得他是哪年畢的業。讓我想一想，對了，
　　大概是一九六〇吧。

18.他的國語說得非常好，簡直的跟北jīng人說得一樣。

19.我希望我的國語說得跟他一樣好。

20.要是我有機會到北jīng去，我一定到你家去看你。

21.到上海去的飛機已經來了嗎？在這兒停幾分鐘？

22.就停十分鐘嗎？我還沒買票呢！我得立刻就走。

23.我不着急。這是我第一次坐飛機。我的皮包在哪
　　兒呢？

24.我知道坐飛機不能帶太多行李，所以我一共就帶
　　兩個小皮包。

25.這個皮包是我自己的，那個皮包是我姐姐讓我替他帶去的。

26.我不知道從這兒到<u>上海</u>得幾個鐘頭。要是哪兒都不停大概半天就可以到了。

27.你的飛機甚麼時候起飛？你怎麼一點兒也不着急呢？

28.你已經買飛機票了嗎？我以為你還沒買呢。

29.票房的門大概已經開了，我眞立刻得走了。

30.希望有機會再跟你談談，再見，一路平安。

Vocabulary

New characters:

記 非 飛 機 清
楚 立 語 讓 急
簡 午 零 停 皮
包 汽 票 希 望

---

1. 記得　　JÌDE　　　　　　FV: remember
　　記　　JÌ　　　　　　　　remember, recollect
2. 天jing　TYĀNJING/tiānjing PW: Tientsin, port city
　　　　　　　　　　　　　　　in Northern China
3. 非常　　FĒICHǍNG　　　　A: very, extraordinarily
　　非　　FĒI　　　　　　　be not
4. 飛機　　FĒIJĪ　　　　　　N: airplane
　　飛　　FĒI　　　　　　　FV: fly
　　機　　JĪ　　　　　　　　machine, opportune
5. 清楚　　CHĪNGCHU/qīngchu SV: be clear
　　清　　CHĪNG/qīng　　　be clear, pure, lucid
　　楚　　CHǓ　　　　　　　clear, orderly
6. 立刻　　LÌKÈ　　　　　　A: at once
　　立　　LÌ　　　　　　　　stand, establish
7. 電話　　DYÀNHWÀ/diànhuà N: telephone
8. 國語　　GWÓYǓ/guóyǔ　　N: (Chinese) national
　　　　　　　　　　　　　　language, Mandarin
　　語　　YǓ　　　　　　　language; a set phrase

9. 讓　　　　RÀNG　　　　CV: let, allow, by (in passive contruction patterns)

10. 急　　　　JÍ　　　　SV: be anxious, hurried, hasty

11. 簡直　　　JYǍNJŕ/JIǍNZHÍ　A: simply

　　　簡　　　JYǍN/jiǎn　　be simple, concise

12. 上午　　　SHÀNGWǓ　　TW: forenoon, morning

　　　午　　　WǓ　　　　noon

13. 特別快車　TÈBYEKUÀICHĒ　N: express train
　　　　　　　tèbiekùaichē

14. 十點零五分　SHŕDIǍN LÍNGWǓFĒN　five minutes past ten
　　　零　　　LÍNG　　　　NU: zero

15. 停　　　　TÍNG　　　　FV: stop

16. 以爲　　　YǏWÉI　　　FV: suppose, think that, take it

17. 皮包　　　PÍBĀU/pібāo　N: suitcase, briefcase, handbag

　　　皮　　　PÍ　　　　bark, skin, leather, fur, peel outer covering

　　　包　　　BĀU/bāo　　M: parcel, pack, package

18. 汽車　　　CHÌCHĒ/qìchē　N: car, automobile

　　　汽　　　CHÌ/qì　　　steam

19. 票　　　　PYÀU/piào　　N: ticket

20. 票房　　　PYÀUFÁNG/piàofáng　N: ticket office

21. nùng錯了　NÙNGTSWÒLE/nòngcùole PH: made a mistake

22. 希望　　　SYĪWÀNG/xīwàng　FV/N: hope

　　　希　　　XĪ　　　　hope

　　　望　　　WÀNG　　　hope, expect, look at

23. 起飛　　　CHǏFĒI/qǐfēi　FV: take off (of a plane)

24. 機會　　　JĪHWEI/jīhui　N: opportunity

25. 着急　　　JĀUJÍ/zhāojí　SV: be worried, get excited

LESSON 4

Characters	Explanations	Expressions
德	*DÉ* BF: Germany	德國 PW: Germany 德法兩國 the two countries: Germany and France
鞋	*SYÉ* N: shoe *xié*	皮鞋 N: leather shoes
號 号	*HÀU* M: day (of month), *hào* number (of house, room, telephone, etc.)	一月一號 January the first 十四街 三百號 #300 14th Street 電話號儿 N: telephone number
顏 颜	*YÁN* BF: color; a surname	顏色 N: color; a surname 姓顏 surnamed Yen
色	*SÈ* BF: color	顏色 N: color

36

Characters	Explanations	Expressions
深	*SHĒN* SV: be deep (color, water, thought)	深顏色 N: deep color 河太深 river is too deep
黄	*HWÁNG* be yellow huáng	深黃 N: deep yellow 黃皮鞋 N: brown shoes
紅 红	*HÚNG* SV: be red húng	紅顏色 N: red color 臉紅了 Ph: blushing
布	*BÙ* N: cotton cloth	布鞋 N: cotton cloth shoes 布作的 Ph: made of cotton
成	*CHÉNG* SV/V/RVE: be O.K., be satisfactory/ become/to complete	成了成? O.K.? 成甚麼了? Ph: become what?

Characters	Explanations	Expressions
換	*HWÀN* huàn V: exchange, change	換錢 VO: exchange money 換東西 VO: change things
淺 浅	*CHYĂN* qiǎn be light (in color), shallow (of water, thought)	淺紅 N: light red 水很淺 Ph: water is shallow 意思很淺 meaning is clear
試 试	*SHÌ* shì V: try	試一試 V: try 說說試試 Ph: try to say it
合	*HÉ* V: join	合適 SV: be suitable, fit 合作 V/N: co-operate/ cooperation 合意 SV: agreeable
適 适	*SHÌ* shì BF: be suitable, fit	合適 SV: be suitable, fit 適當 shrdàng SV: suitable, fit

Characters	Explanations	Expressions

量	*LYÀNG* V: measure
	liàng
		商量 shānglyang
		    V: discuss,
		      talk over
		
		量量 lyángryang
		    V: measure

式	*SHR̀* BF: style, pattern, *shì* fashion	中式 N: Chinese style 西式 N: western style or fashion 新式 SV: be modern 舊式 SV: be old fashioned 式樣 N: style
價 价	*JYÀ* BF: price, cost *jià*	價錢 N: price, cost

商	*SHĀNG* trade, commerce	商量 shānglyang
		    V: discuss, talk
		      over
		
		商業 N: business, trade,
		      commerce
		商人 N: a merchant

樓 楼	*LÓU* N/M: storied building (orig. an upper story)/(for floors)	樓上 N: upstairs 二樓 N: second floor

第四kè gù 事

小王在城裏買了一shwāng[1] 黑顏色[2]的布鞋[3]，一打[4]黃顏色的 wà[5] 子，跟一件深顏色的大衣[6]。回到張家[7]，就把那些東西給張太太，張小姐看，問他們樣子跟顏色好不好，價錢[9]貴不貴。張小姐看見了這些東西，笑着對小王說：「不成[10]，不成。」

小王不懂那是甚麼意思，就問張小姐爲甚麼不成。張小姐說：

「現在的學生多半兒[11]穿皮鞋[12]，你爲甚麼買布鞋呢？這一打wà子的顏色也不對，大衣的樣子也太舊，不成，不成，都不成，最好立刻拿回去換[13]。」

小王說：「可是我不知道甚麼顏色好，甚麼樣子新式[14]。」

張小姐說：「城裏電報局的後頭有一個鋪子，我可以給你介紹，那兒的鞋的顏色跟樣子都好。」

小王說：「可是我不知道怎麼去。」

「你明天跟我一塊兒去吧。」張小姐說。

第二天張小姐帶着小王到那個鋪子的二樓去[15]。張小姐對小王說：

「皮鞋一定要買德國[16]作的，我看那shwāng淺黃[17]顏色的皮鞋樣子很不錯，你試試[18]，覺得怎麼樣？」

小王試了試，說:「大小[19]很合適[20]，可是顏色太淺了一點兒。」

張小姐說:「夏天應當穿淺顏色的，我看很合適。」

張小姐問小王喜歡穿甚麼顏色的wà子。小王說:「黑顏色的不錯。」

張小姐說:「黑顏色的wà子是鄉下人穿的。我看你最好穿深紅顏色的。這是十一號[21]，你試試[22]，成不成。」

張小姐又帶小王到三樓試大衣。

張小姐說:「大衣應當買yīng國作的。你試試這一件淺顏色的吧。」

小王說:「很合適，可是價錢……」

張小姐說:「貴的不貴，jyàn的不jyàn[23]，我看這一件的樣子不錯，你就買這一件吧。」

回了家，張小姐對小王說:「你以後要買甚麼東西都可以跟我商量[24]。」

小王說:「一定，一定。」

第四 kè　　句　子

1. 我去年春天到<u>德國</u>去旅行的時候，我到一個鞋鋪去買鞋。

2. 鋪子裏的人問我穿幾號的鞋。喜歡甚麼顏色。

3. 我告訴他我要買一 shwāng 深黃的皮鞋，可是我不記得穿幾號的鞋。

4. 因爲我的<u>德國</u>話說得不太好，所以他沒聽清楚。

5. 他給了我一 shwāng 深紅的皮鞋。我說:「不成，不成。」

6. 他給我換了一 shwāng 淺紅的布鞋，我還說:「不成，不成。」

7. 我說，我要深黃的皮鞋，不要淺紅的布鞋。

8. 後來他聽清楚了。他給我換了一 shwāng 深黃的皮鞋，要我試一試。

9. 我試了試，覺得不合適。我問他那 shwāng 鞋幾號。他說六號。

10. 我說六號的不合適，請你給我換一 shwāng 七號的吧。

11. 他給我換了一 shwāng 七號的，可是我還覺得不合適。

12.後來他量了量我的jyǎu， 他說，我應當穿六號半
　　的鞋。

13.我試了試六號半的，覺得很合適。我說:「成，六
　　號半的很合適。」

14.可是我不喜歡這個鞋的樣子。他說這是最新式的
　　皮鞋。

15.我問他價錢貴不貴。他說:「價錢不貴，價錢不貴。」

16.我回國以後，我的朋友都說，我鞋的樣子好。

17.很多人跟我商量，要我替他們買鞋。

18.我說我有一個朋友姓<u>李</u>，他是一個<u>德國</u>的商人，
　　我可以跟他商量，請他替你們買。

19.我給<u>李</u>先生寫了一封航空信，請他替我的朋友買
　　鞋。

20.<u>李</u>先生說:「成，可是你得告訴我那個鞋鋪在哪兒。」

21.我又給他寫了一封航空信說:「鞋鋪在郵局的前頭，
　　樓上是旅館，樓下是鞋鋪。」

22.他問我:「一共要幾shwāng? 甚麼顏色？幾號？」

23.我說:「一共要買兩shwāng， 一shwāng皮鞋 ， 一
　　shwāng布鞋。

24.皮鞋請買七號，深紅的; 布鞋請買六號，淺黃的。」

25.那年的秋天我接着李先生的一封信，信上說:「鞋
已經寄走了，請你們收到以後立刻試一試，要
是不合適可以寄回來換。」

26.我們收到鞋以後大家都試了，都覺得很合適。

27.大家都說德國鞋真不錯，樣子好，價錢也不貴。

28.後來又有很多朋友要我給他們介紹李先生。

29.我說:「不成，買鞋的人太多了，李先生恐怕不願
意幫忙。

30.我給你們介紹那個鞋鋪，你們自已給那個鞋鋪寫
信吧。」

Vocabulary

New characters:

顏　色　布　鞋　黃
深　價　成　換　式
樓　德　淺　試　合
適　紅　號　商　量

---

1. shwāng   /shūang   M: *pair (for shoes, socks, etc.*
2. 顏色   YÁNSÈ/yénsè   N: *color*
   顏   YÁN   *color*
   色   SÈ   *color*
3. 布鞋   BÙSYÉ/bùxié   N: *cotton shoes*
   布   BÙ   N: *cotton cloth*
   鞋   SYÉ/xié   N: *shoe*
4. 一打   YÌDÁ   M: *one dozen*
5. 黃   HWÁNG/huáng   SV: *be yellow*
6. wà 子   WÀDZ /wàzi   N: *sock*
7. 深   SHĒN   SV: *be deep (color, water,*
8. 大衣   DÀYĪ   N: *overcoat*   *thought)*
9. 價錢   JYÀCHYÁN/jiàqián   N: *price, cost*
   價   JYÀ/jià   *price, cost*
10. 成   CHÉNG   SV: *be satisfactory, O.K.*
11. 多半兒   DWŌBÀR/duōbàr   A: *majority, most of*
12. 皮鞋   PÍSYÉ/píxié   N: *leather shoes*

13. 換   HWÀN/huàn   FV: exchange, change

14. 新式   SYĪNSHR/xīnshì SV: be modern

    式   SHR̀/shì   style, pattern, fashion

15. 二樓   ÈRLÓU   N: second floor

    樓   LÓU   N/M: storied building/(floors)

16. 德國   DÉGWO/déguo   PW: Germany

    德   DÉ   Germany; virtue

17. 淺黃   CHYǍNHWÁNG   N: light yellow
               qiǎnhuáng   SV: be light(in color); shallow

    淺   (of water, thought)

18. 試試   SHR̀SHR/shìshi FV: try

    試   SHR̀/shì   FV: try

19. 大小   DÀSYǍU/dàxiǎo N: size

20. 合適   HÉSHR/héshì   SV: be suitable

    合   HÉ   FV: join

    適   SHR̀/shì   be suitable, fit

21. 紅   HÚNG/hóng   SV: be red

22. 號   HÀU/hào   M: size; day (of month);
                                  number (of house, room, etc.)

23. "貴的不貴   GWÈIDE BÚGWÈI, JYÀNDE BÚJYÀN/gùide búgùi
    jyàn的不   jiànde bújiàn. PH:"You get what you pay
    jyàn"   for."

24. 商量   SHĀNGLYANG/shāngliang FV: discuss, talk over

    商   SHĀNG   discuss; trade, commerce

    量   LYÀNG/liàng   estimate; think

25. 量   LYÁNG/liáng   FV: measure

26. jyǎu   jiǎo   N: foot

27. 商人   SHĀNGREN   M: merchant

28. 寄走了   JÌDZŎULE/jìzǒule   *RV: mailed out*

29. 收到   SHŌUDÀU/shōudào   *RV: receive*

LESSON 5

Characters	Explanations	Expressions
烟	*YĀN* N: tobacco, cigarette; smoke	一包烟 N: a pack of cigarettes 烟太多 Ph: too much smoke
租	*DZŪ* V: rent zū	租房子 VO: rent a house 房租 N: house rent 租錢 N: rental 租汽車 VO: rent a car 出租 V: for rent
雖 虽	*SWĒI* BF: although suī	雖然 A: although
單 单	*DĀN* BF: be simple; odd (as a number)	簡單 SV: be simple (opp. complex) 單子 N: list 菜單子 N: menu
結 结	*JYÉ* BF: unite, connect jié	結婚 VO: get married, marriage

48

Characters	Explanations	Expressions
婚	*HWŪN* BF: marriage *hūn*	結婚　VO: get married, 　　　　　marriage 離婚　VO: divorce 結婚禮　N: marriage 　　　　　ceremony
像	*SYÀNG* SV: resemble, seem *xiàng*　　　 like/look alike	好像　V/A: resemble/a 　　　　　good deal 　　　　　like, just 　　　　　as though, 　　　　　it seem that 像誰　like whom? 不像　not at all like
係　系	*SYÌ* BF: belong to *xì*	關係　N: relation, 　　　　　connection, 　　　　　relevance 沒關係　Ph: unrelated, 　　　　　irrelevant, 　　　　　it doesn't 　　　　　matter
聲　声	*SHĒNG* BF: sound, voice	聲音　N: voice, noise, 　　　　　sound 大聲說　Ph: speak loudly
音	*YĪN* BF: sound	聲音　N: voice, noise, 　　　　　sound

Characters	Explanations	Expressions
按	ÀN CV: according to	按我的意思 in my opinion 按月算 Ph: calculate according to month
管	GWĂN guǎn manage, take care of, attend to/ tube, pipe	管子 N: tube, pipe 不管 V: don't care whether, no matter whether 管不着 IE: none of one's business 管燈水 include electricity and water
燈 灯	DĒNG N: lamp, light, lantern	電燈 N: electric light 手電燈 N: flashlight
久	JYŎU SV: for a long time jiǔ	很久沒見 IE: "Long time no see." 不久 MA: before long
需	SYŪ BF: need xū	需要 BF: need 必需 AV: must

Characters	Explanations	Expressions
牆	*CHYÁNG* n. wall *qiáng*	牆上 PW: on the wall
暫 暂	*JÀN* **BF:** briefly, shortly, *zhàn* temporarily	暫時 MA: temporarily
決	*JYWÉ* **BF:** decide, decidedly *jué*	決定 V: decide 決不去 Ph: definitely will not go
留	*LYÓU* **V:** keep, detain, *líu* preserve	留定錢 VO: leave a deposit 留學 V: study abroad 留學生 N: students abroad 留下 RV: leave it here
廣 广	*GWĂNG* *sv: be broad* *guǎng*	廣告 N: advertisement

第五kè　gù 事

　　小王在張家住了差不多兩個禮拜，覺得在那兒
住有很多事情不方便，所以想到別的地方去租一間
房間，自己一個人住。他在報上看見了一個廣告，
有一間房間出租，離學校就有半里路，房租也不貴。
小王覺得很合適，所以就坐着汽車到那個房子那兒
去了。

　　小王見了房東說:「我在報上看見你那個房間出
租的廣告了。請問是甚麼樣兒的房間？我能不能看
一看？」

　　那個房東是一個四十幾歲的老太太。他看了看
小王說:

　　「你是不是北海大學的學生？我這間房間就租給
北海大學的學生。」

　　小王說:「我是剛從上海來的，今年秋天打算進
北海大學。

　　房東說:「你結婚了沒有？有沒有孩子？我這兒
不租給結婚的人。」

　　「我沒結婚。」

「請進來吧。」房東說。

那間房間在二樓，不很大。屋子裏的東西雖然簡單[10]，可是很乾淨。房租按月算，每月三十塊錢[11]，管燈，水[12]。

房東說:「這兒住的人不可以chōu烟[13]，不可以喝酒。」

小王說:「沒有關係[14]，我不chōu烟也不喝酒。」

「不可以大聲說話[15]，屋子裏不可以作飯。」

「這也沒有關係，我說話的聲音[16]不大，我也不想作飯。」

「夜裏十點鐘以後不可以開燈[17]，屋子得收拾得很乾淨。」房東接着[18]說。

小王說:「我暫時[19]不能決定[20]，讓我跟朋友商量商量。我給你留五塊錢的定錢[21]，你給我留兩天[22]，成不成？」

房東說:「成，可是現在要租房的學生很多。像這樣的屋子一定有很多人要租，所以我不能給你留太久[23][24]。要是明天中午你不來，我就租給別人了。」

小王回去以後就跟張家商量。張小姐說:「像這樣的房東，要是我是你，我一定不住他的

房子。」

　　張太太說:「你在這兒住吧，不必客氣。」

　　張先生也說:「你暫時在這兒住幾個禮拜，秋天以後你可以住在學校裏，那兒又便yi又乾淨。」

　　「可是你的定錢怎麼辦？」張小姐問。

　　「沒有關係。」小王說,「小李也想找房，我明天告訴他，讓他去看看吧。」

第五kè　　句　子

1. 謝謝你，我不chōu 烟。你剛才說你要租房嗎？我現在住的那所房²⁵可以讓你住。

2. 我今年冬天就要畢業了，畢業以後想到德國去留學²⁶。

3. 那所房在鄉下，離這兒大概有十里路。

4. 前頭是海，後頭是山。房子雖然不大，可是風景很好。

5. 夏天一點兒不熱，晚上，海上的風特別大。

6. 一共有四間屋子，樓上兩間，樓下兩間，房子裏的東西很簡單，可是很新。

7. 你結婚了沒有？像這樣的房子給結婚的人住，合適極了。

8. 你跟你太太離婚²⁷了嗎？沒有關係，那位房東也離過一次婚。

9. 屋裏當然可以chōu 烟。孩子說話的聲音大也沒有關係。

10. 房租按月算。按禮拜算都可以。要是按月算，每月六十塊錢。

11.不管燈，水。燈，水每月大概十塊錢。

12.你打算在這兒住多久，要是住得很久，房租也許
　　可以少一點兒。

13 你得跟房東談一談。你需要甚麼可以告訴他。

14.要是你開汽車去半個鐘頭就到了。房子的牆是紅
　　顏色的，很容易找。

15.你暫時不能決定嗎？沒有關係，你不管甚麼時候
　　決定都成。

16.你可以先留一點兒定錢，請他給你留一個禮拜。

17.報上的房子出租廣告雖然很多，可是像那樣合適
　　的房子很少。

18.我租那所房子的時候，是看見了廣告才找着的。

19.我看見的不是報上的廣告，是牆上的廣告。

20.那天我在鄉下玩兒，看見牆上有一張房子出租的
　　廣告。

21.按那個地方的人說，那所房子已經很久沒租出去
　　了。

22.我見了房東，房東說，那所房子暫時不能住，因
　　為水管子跟電燈都還沒收拾好。

23.我說，我已經決定租那所房子了，不管有沒有燈，

水我都得租。

24.我立刻留了二十塊錢的定錢。雖然房東說不需要留定錢，可是我還是留了。

25.房東說:「這個房子裏的東西很簡單，你需要甚麼東西可以跟我說。」

26.我說:「我暫時不需要甚麼，要是以後我需要甚麼，我一定告訴你。」

27.我在那兒住了很久。我希望這次到德國去留學能找到像這樣的房子。

28.我決定十一月一號上午坐十點零五分的飛機到德國去。

29.我走以前你們可以暫時住幾個月的旅館。

30.那位房東雖然是上海人，可是國語說得很好。你跟他說話的時候聲音得大一點兒。

Vocabulary

New characters:

租　廣　結　婚　雖
單　按　管　燈　烟
係　聲　音　暫　決
留　像　久　需　牆

---

1. 租　　　　DZŪ/zū　　　FV: rent

2. 房間　　　FÁNGJYĀN/fángjiān N: room

3. 廣告　　　GWǍNGGÀU/guǎnggào N: advertisement

　　廣　　　GWǍNG/guǎng　SV: be broad

4. 出租　　　CHŪDZŪ/chūzū　FV: for rent

5. 房租　　　FÁNGDZŪ/fángzū N: house rent

6. 房東　　　FÁNGDŪNG/fángdōng N: landlord; landlady

7. 租給　　　DZŪGĚI/zūgěi　FV: rent (it) to

　　V 給　　Verb - gěi　　verb - to

8. 結婚　　　JYÉHWŪN/jiéhūn VO: get married; marriage

　　結　　　JYÉ/jié　　　unite; connect

　　婚　　　HWŪN/hūn　　marriage

9. 雖然　　　SWĒIRÁN/suírán A: although

　　雖　　　SWĒI/suí　　　although

10. 簡單　　JYǍNDĀN/jiǎndān SV: be simple

　　單　　　DĀN　　　　simple

11. 按月算　ÀNYWÈ SWÀN　PH: figure according to
　　　　　　ànyuè suàn　　　the month

	按	ÀN	CV: according to
12.	管燈水	GWǍN DĒNG-SHWĔI gǔan dēng-shǔi	PH: including water and electricity
	管	GWǍN/gǔan	FV: take care of, manage
	燈	DĒNG	N: lamp, light
13.	chōu烟	CHŌUYĀN	VO: smoke
	烟	YĀN	N: tobacco, cigarette smoke
14.	沒有關係	MÉIYOU GWĀNSYI méiyou gūanxi	PH: it doesn9t matter
	關係		N: relation
	係	SYÌ/xì	belong to
15.	大聲說話	DÀSHĒNG SHWŌHWÀ dàshēng shūohùa	PH: to speak loudly
	聲	SHĒNG	voice, sound
16.	聲音	SHĒNGYIN	N: voice, sound, noise
	音	YĪN	sound
17.	開燈	KĀIDĒNG	VO: turn on the lights
18.	接着	JYĒJE/jiēzhe	A: continue, go on
19.	暫時	JÀNSHŔ/zhànshí	MA: temporarily
	暫	JÀN/zhàn	temporarily
20.	決定	JYWÉDÌNG/juédìng	FV: decide
	決	JYWÉ/jué	decide
21.	留定錢	LYÓU DÌNGCHYÁN líu dìngqían	FV: leave a deposit
	留	LYÓU/líu	FV: keep, leave
22.	留兩天	LYÓU LYĂNGTYĀN líu liǎngtīan	PH: keep for 2 days
23.	像	SYÀNG/xìang	SV: be like, resemble
24.	久	JYǑU/jǐu	SV: long time
25.	所	SWǑ/sǒ	M: (for houses)
26.	留學	LYÓUSYWÉ/líuxué	FV: study abroad
27.	離婚	LÍHWŪN/líhūn	VO: divorce

28. 多久   DWŌJYǑU/dūojǐu   A/SV: how long (time)?
29. 需要   SYŪYÀU/xūyào   FV/N: need
    需   SYŪ/xū   need
30. 牆   CHYÁNG/qiáng   N: wall
31. 水管子   SHWĔIGWǍNDZ   N: water pipe
32. 電燈   shúiguǎnzi
             DYÀNDĒNG/diàndēng N: electric light
33. 不管...   BÙGWǍN ... DŌU
    (都)...   bùguǎn ... dōu   PH: do not care whether ...
                                       no matter whether ...

LESSON 6

Characters	Explanations	Expressions
警	*JĬNG* BF: to warn, to caution	警察 N: policeman 警察局 N: police department 警告 V/N: warn/warning 警報 N: alarm
察	*CHÁ* BF: find out	警察 N: policeman 警察局 N: police department
賊 賊	*DZÉI* N: thief *zéi*	作賊 VO: be a thief 有賊 thief! thief!
偷	*TŌU* V: steal	偷偷的 A: stealthily, secretly 偷東西 VO: steal things
派	*PÀI* V: appoint, send (someone to do something)	派人 VO: send someone 派他去 Ph: send him

Characters	Explanations	Expressions
保	*BĂU* BF: protect *bǎo*	保險 VO: take insurance
險 险	*SYĂN* SV: be dangerous, *xiǎn* perilous	保險 VO: take insurance
金	*JĪN* BF: gold	金子 N: gold 美金 N: American money (gold) 金表 N: gold watch
銀 银	*YÍN* BF: silver	銀子 N: silver 銀行 yínháng N: bank 銀子作的 Ph: made of silver

該 该	*GĀI* AV/V: ought, should/owe	應該 AV: should, ought
		      (interchangeable
		      with 應當
		該誰 Ph: whose turn?

Characters	Explanations	Expressions
取	*CHYÜ* / *qǔ* V: fetch (things), take out	取錢 VO: fetch money, withdraw money 取東西 VO: fetch things
敢	*GĂN* AV: dare, venture	不敢當 IE: you flatter me (lit. I dare not assume the honor.) 敢説 Ph: sure (of one's facts)
除	*CHÚ* CV: deduct/besides, except	除了……以外 in addition to...., besides; except
另	*LING* SP: another, besides, in addition	另外 SP/MA: another/ besides, in addition
銅 / 铜	*TÚNG* / *tóng* N: copper, brass	銅的 N: of copper, of brass 黃銅 N: brass 紅銅 N: copper

Characters	Explanations	Expressions
值 值 alternate	*JŔ* *zhí* V: be worth (so much)	值錢 VO/SV: be worth (so much) money/ be valuable 值得 AV: worth while 價值 N: value
嗎 吗	*MA* P: (question particle)	你好嗎? How are you?
公	*GŪNG* BF: public official *gōng*	公里 M: a kilometer 公共汽車 N: bus 公立學校 N: publicly established school
司	*SZ̄* BF: [L. be in charge of] *sī*	公司 N: company, corporation
實 实	*SHŔ* BF: be real, true; *shí* solid	結實 jyēshr SV: be strong, durable, sturdy 實在 SV/A: be real, honest/really, actually

第六kè　　gù 事

　　有一天小王請張小姐出去玩兒，他們回家的時候已經快夜裏十二點鐘了。小王對張小姐說：

　　「你父母大概已經睡了。」

　　張小姐說：「大概是，我們應當小聲[1]一點兒走路，別開燈了。」

　　小王慢慢兒的[2]把大門開開。他們兩個人 twŏ[3] 了皮鞋，偷偷兒的[4]往房子裏走。

　　那個時候張先生跟張太太都還沒睡着呢。他們聽見開門的聲音，就到chwāng hu前頭去看。可是外頭非常黑，所以看不清楚甚麼東西。他們就看見有兩個人偷偷兒的進來了。張先生跟張太太說：

　　「也許是賊[5]來偷[6]東西來了，讓我出去看看吧。」

　　「別出去，」張太太很着急的說，「那兩個賊，有一個長的[7]又高又大，一定也比你結實。你爲甚麼不給[8]警察局打電話呢？」

　　張先生聽了立刻給警察局打了一個電話，告訴他們家裏有賊，請他們派[10]幾個警察[9]來。張先生打了電話就問張太太說：

「我今天從銀行裏取回來的一百塊美金，你放在哪兒了？」

「我放在我的皮包裏了。」張太太說。

「客 tīng 裏除了幾個金子作的 wǎn 以外，另外還有值錢的東西沒有？」

張太太說：「除了那些金 wǎn 以外別的東西都是銅作的，不值甚麼錢。別着急，那些金 wǎn 都保了險了。」

小王跟張小姐正說着再見呢，大門外頭來了很多警察。那個時候張先生，張太太也從房子裏出來了。他們看見是小王跟他們的女兒，知道 nùng 錯了。張先生對警察說：

「實在對不起，我們 nùng 錯了。」

張小姐說：「這都是小王的錯兒。」

小王想說幾句話，可是他不知道應該說甚麼。後來張先生說：

「時候不早了，大家都去睡吧。」

第六kè　　句　子

1.我得立刻到警察局去。我家昨天夜裏來了一個賊,
　偷了很多東西去。

2.你爲甚麼不給警察局打一個電話, 請他們派一個
　警察來呢?

3.好, 可是我記不清楚警察局的電話多少號了。

4.那個賊偷了一些甚麼東西, 那些東西都保險了沒
　有?

5.那個賊偷了我一個金表, 一個皮包, 一shwāng淺
　黃顏色的皮鞋, 還有很多銀的東西。

6.你不應該把金的跟銀的東西放在家裏, 你爲甚麼
　不放在銀行裏呢?

7.本來是放在銀行裏的, 昨天才取出來。我以爲警
　察局離我家不到一公里路, 一定沒有賊敢來偷
　東西。

8.除了那些金的, 銀的東西以外還偷了別的東西沒
　有?

9.還有一些銅的東西, 不值甚麼錢, 最值錢的是那
　個金表。

10.是一個甚麼樣的金表?值多少錢?

11.那個表是我姐姐的，是一個<u>德國</u>表，五年以前值
　　兩百塊美金，現在的價錢當然比以前貴多了。

12.我剛才給我姐姐寫了一封航空信，可是還沒寄呢。

13.我回去的時候我的汽車可以在郵局停一停，替你
　　去寄那封航空信。

14.你那些東西都保險了吧？你給保險公司²⁶打電話了
　　嗎²⁷？

15.我剛才給保險公司打電話了，他們要我把偷了的
　　東西開一張單子²⁸，等一會兒他們就派人來。

16.你應該開兩張單子，一張給保險公司，一張給警
　　察局。

17.單子已經開好了，可是有很多東西的價錢我記不
　　清楚了。

18.那個賊進來的時候你已經睡着了嗎？

19.那個賊大概是夜裏十一點鐘進來的。那個時候我
　　還沒睡着。

20.我看見一個穿深黃衣 shang 的人從chwānghu 那兒
　　進來。

21.你看見那個賊進來，爲甚麼不大聲叫呢？

22.因爲我看見那個賊比我高，也比我結實，所以我

沒敢叫。

23.那個賊非常客氣的警告我說:「我來取一點兒東西，
　　請不要怕，也不要大聲叫。」

24.我說，這兒實在沒有甚麼值錢的東西，卓子上的
　　那些東西都是銅作的。」

25.他說,「沒有關係，銅作的東西很結實，比金子作
　　的好。」

26.他看了看我姐姐的那個德國表說:「這個表很值錢
　　吧？」

27.我說:「這是一個舊式的表，不值甚麼錢，你拿另
　　外那個銀的吧。」

28.他說:「除了這個金表以外，你還有一個銀的嗎？
　　好極了，我都要。」

29.他走的時候說:「我取的東西你都記清楚了嗎？明
　　天你可以告訴保險公司，跟公司要錢。」

30.他走了以後我不敢起來，也不敢給警察局打電話。
　　我恐怕他還在門外頭等着我呢。

Vocabulary

New characters:

偷　賊　實　警　察
派　銀　取　金　除
另　值　銅　保　險
該　敢　公　司　嗎

---

1. 小聲　　　　SYĀUSHĒNG/xiǎoshēng A: quietly, in a
                                            low voice
2. 慢慢兒的　　MÀNMĀNRDE　　A: slowly
3. ｔ wō　　　　TWŌ/tuō　　　FV: take off (clothes)
4. 偷偷兒的　　TŌUTŌURDE　　A: secretly, stealthily
5. 賊　　　　　DZÉI/zéi　　　N: thief, burglar
6. 偷　　　　　TŌU　　　　　FV: steal
7. 長的　　　　JǍNGDE/zhǎngde　FV: grow
8. 結實　　　　JYÉSHR/jiēshi　SV: be strong
   實　　　　　SHŔ/shí　　　　　solid, real
9. 警察局　　　JǏNGCHÁJYÚ/jǐngchájú N: police dept.
   警　　　　　JǏNG　　　　　warn, caution
   察　　　　　CHÁ　　　　　find out
10. 派　　　　　PÀI　　　　　FV: send (someone)
11. 銀行　　　　YÍNHÁNG　　　N: bank
    銀　　　　　YÍN　　　　　silver
12. 取　　　　　CHYǓ/qǔ　　　FV: take out; fetch, go get
13. 美金　　　　MĚIJĪN　　　　N: United States currency

	金	JĪN	gold
14.	除了…以外	CHÚLE .. YÍWÀI	PAT: in addition to ... besides ... , except ...
	除	CHÚ	deduct
15.	金子	JĪNDZ/jīnzi	N: gold
16.	另外	LÌNGWÀI	MA: besides, in addition
	另	LÌNG	another
17.	值錢	JŔCHYÁN/zhíqián	VO/SV: be worth/be valuable (in money)
	值	JŔ/zhí	FV: be worth
18.	銅	TÚNG/tóng	N: copper, brass
19.	保險	BĂUSYĂN/băoxiăn	VO: take insurance
	保	BĂU/băo	protect against
	險	SYĂN/xiăn	danger
20.	實在	SHŔDZÀI/shízài	SV/A: be real; really
21.	錯兒	TSWÒR/cuòr	N: fault, mistake
22.	應該	YĪNGGĀI	AV: should, ought
	該	GĀI	AV: should, ought
23.	不到	BÚDÀU/búdào	FV: less than, not quite
24.	公里	GŪNGLĬ/gōnglǐ	M: kilometer
	公	GŪNG/gōng	public; official
25.	敢	GĂN	AV: dare, venture to
26.	保險	BĂUSYĂN/băoxiăn	N: insurance
	公司	GŪNGSZ̄/gōngsī	N: company
	司	SZ̄/sī	manage
27.	嗎	MA	P: (question particle)
28.	開單子	KĀI DĀNDZ/kāi dānzi	VO: make out a list
	單子	DĀNDZ/dānzi	N: list

29. 警告   *JǐNGGÀU/jǐnggào*   FV/N: *warn; warning*
30. 舊式   *JYÒUSHR̀/jiùshì*   SV: *be old fashioned*

LESSON 7

Characters	Explanations	Expressions
死	*SŽ* / *sǐ* V: die, be dead	死人 N: dead person
活	*HWÓ* / *huó* V: be alive [SV: moveable]	生活 V/N: live/livelihood, living
堂	*TÁNG* BF: hall, room	教堂 N: church (building) 大禮堂 N: auditorium
世	*SHR̀* / *shì* BF: world	世界 N: the world
界	*JYÈ* / *jiè* BF: boundary	世界 N: the world 邊界 N: border

73

Characters	Explanations	Expressions
理	*LǏ* V/N: regard, pay attention/reason, the fitness of things	道理 N: teaching, doctrine 有理 VO/SV: logical, reasonable 地理 N: geography 不理 V: pay no attention; do not talk to
研 研	*YÁN* BF: investigate thoroughly, research	研究 V/N: research, study
究	*JYŌU* BF: examine into *jiū*	研究 V/N: research, study
滿 满	*MǍN* SV: to be full	坐滿了 RV: all seats are taken, (the room) is full
講 讲	*JYǍNG* V: explain, talk *jiǎng*	講書 VO: explain the lesson, lecture (in class) 講話 VO: speak 講道 VO: preach

Characters	Explanations	Expressions
苦	*KǓ* SV: be bitter to the taste; be hard, difficult (of life)	吃苦 VO: suffer bitterly
窮 穷	*CHYÚNG* qióng : be poor	窮人 N: poor people
星	*SYĪNG* xīng BF: star	星星 N: star
期	*CHĪ* qī BF: period, date, limit of time	星期 N: week
反	*FǍN* BF: oppose, turn back, be contrary to, the wrong side	反正 MA: in any case, anyway (right or wrong) 反對 V: oppose

Characters	Explanations	Expressions
興 兴	*SYÌNG* *xìng* interest, excitement	高興 SV: be happy, in high spirits
低	*DĪ* SV/V: be low/lower	低頭 VO: bow the head
故	*GÙ* BF: reason, cause, old, ancient	故事 N: story
静	*JÌNG* SV: be quiet	安静 SV: be quiet
約 约	*YWĒ* *yūe* V: invite, make an appointment	約會 N: engagement, appointment

第七kè　故事

　　張小姐信jīdū敎，他每星期日早上都到敎堂去作禮拜。有一天張小姐問小王信甚麼敎。小王說，他甚麼敎都不信，他覺得世界上沒有上dì。張小姐聽了他的話，很不高興的說：

　　「你沒有研究過jīdū敎的道理，怎麼知道沒有上dì呢？」

　　小王說：「那麼請你給我講一講jīdū敎的道理吧。」

　　「jīdū敎的道理不那麼簡單，我說不清楚。這星期日你爲甚麼不跟我到敎堂去作禮拜呢？」

　　「好是好，不過這個星期日我跟小李有一個約會。」

　　「那沒有關係，」張小姐說，「你爲甚麼不請小李跟我們一塊兒去呢？」

　　小王沒有法子，就給小李打了一個電話，問小李願意不願意去作禮拜去。

　　小李說：「我不信敎，爲甚麼去作禮拜？」

　　小王說：「張小姐要請你去作禮拜，要是你不願意去就算了吧。」

　　「不過，」小李接着說，「聽說jīdū敎的道理很有意

思，反正我沒甚麼事，請你告訴張小姐，我一定去，
我一定去。」

　　星期日早上小王，小李跟張小姐一塊兒去作禮
拜。他們到教堂的時候那兒已經快坐滿了。教堂裡
的人雖然很多，可是很安靜。小王對張小姐說：

　　「你看，前頭有幾個dzwò 位。」

　　張小姐看了看小王說：「請小點兒聲兒說話，別
忘了，這是教堂。」

　　他們坐下以後，不久大家都站起來唱dzàn美shr，
小王跟小李也跟着唱。過了一會兒大家低頭chídǎu，
他們也跟着大家chídǎu。　後來mùshr 講道了，他講
了一個故事。他說：

　　「從前有一個有錢的父親，他有兩個兒子。小兒
子很壞。他拿了他父親的錢，到別的地方去，把錢都
用完了，窮得沒有飯吃，苦極了。後來他覺得自己
不對，所以又回到他父親的家裡去了。他父親看見
小兒子回來了，很高興。大兒子不懂他父親爲甚麼
高興，就去問他父親。他父親說：「你弟弟死了，又
活了，dyōu了，又找回來了。我怎麼能不高興呢？」」

　　作完了禮拜，張小姐問小王，小李覺得怎麼樣。

小王說:「不壞，不壞。」

小李說： 「很有意思， 很有意思。」

第七kè　　句　子

1. 我很久沒看見王先生了。有的人說他已經死了，有的人說他還活着呢。

2. 我第一次看見王先生是在一個教堂裏。一個朋友給我們介紹的。

3. 我覺得他是世界上最奇怪的人，可是他對地理³²很有研究³³。

4. 不管是春天hwò是夏天，他老穿一件舊的布衣shang，從來沒換過。

5. 他住的那間屋子又小又不乾淨，淺紅顏色的牆已經成了黑顏色的了。

6. 桌子上有很多書，那些書多半兒是地理書。

7. 他的生活苦極³⁴了，可是他說，他一點兒也不苦。

8. 我先以爲他很窮，後來我知道他不窮。

9. 有一次我有要緊的事情，得坐飛機到上海去。我需要一百塊錢買飛機票。

10. 可是那天是星期六，銀行不開門，所以我取不着錢。

11. 王先生說：「我這兒有錢，你拿去用吧，反正我暫

時不需要。」

12. 他不高興的時候就低着頭不理人。

13. 他高興的時候就給人講很多故事。

14. 他講的故事都很有道理。有的時候道理太深了我
    就不懂了。

15. 有的時候他低着頭，很靜的，半天不說話，好像
    睡着了一樣。

16. 有的時候我想約他到街上去玩兒。他說街上的人
    太多，不安靜。

17. 有的時候我想約他到上海去旅行。他說火車票太
    貴，他很窮，買不起票。

18. 可是我每次約他到教堂去作禮拜，他都不反對，
    很高興的跟我去。

19. 有一次我問他結婚了沒有。他說結婚了，可是太
    太死了。

20. 我又問他爲甚麼不再結婚。他低着頭，半天沒說
    話。

21. 後來他說，在這個世界上不容易找着一位合適的
    小姐。

22. 我說我可以給他介紹一位合適的小姐。他笑着說，

誰願意跟一個像他那麼窮的人結婚呢。

23.有一個星期日我到教堂去作禮拜，可是那天王先生沒去。

24.我到他家去找他，他沒在家。按房東說，他已經三天沒回家了。

25.春天過去了，夏天也過去了，可是我一直沒再看見過王先生。有的人說他已經死了，有的人說他還活着呢。

26.有一天我在上海鄉下的一個教堂裏作禮拜。那天作禮拜的人很多，教堂裏快坐滿了。

27.我看見一個人很像王先生。我高興極了，想立刻走過去叫他

28.可是教堂裡很安靜，我不能大聲的叫。

29.那個人沒理我，低着頭，從另外的一個門出去了。

30.我真希望有一天王先生會回來給我講很多故事。

Vocabulary

New characters:

星　期　堂　世　界
興　研　究　理　講
約　反　滿　靜　低
故　窮　苦　死　活

---

1. jīdū教　　　　JĪDŪ-JYÀU/jīdūjiào　　N: Christianity
   信教　　　　　SYÌNJYÀU/xìnjiào　　　VO: believe in a religion
   信　　　　　　SYÌN/xìn　　　　　　　FV: believe (in)

2. 星期日　　　SYĪNGCHÍR/xīngqírì　N: Sunday; combines with
   　　　　　　　　　　　　　　　　　numbers one through six for remaining
   　　　　　　　　　　　　　　　　　days of the week. Syīngchīyī, (Monday)
   　　　　　　　　　　　　　　　　　Syīngchīèr (Tuesday), etc.

3. 教堂　　　　JYÀUTÁNG/jiàotáng　　N: church (building)
   堂　　　　　　TÁNG　　　　　　　　hall, room

4. 作禮拜　　　DZWÒLǏBÀI/zuòlǐbài　VO: go to church (services)

5. 世界　　　　SHRJYÈ/shìjiè　　　　N: world
   世　　　　　　SHR/shì　　　　　　　world
   界　　　　　　JYÈ/jiè　　　　　　　boundary

6. 上dì　　　　SHÀNGDÌ　　　　　　　N: God

7. 高興　　　　GĀUSYÌNG/gāoxìng　　SV: be happy
   興　　　　　　SYÌNG/xìng　　　　　interest, excitement

8. 研究　　　　YÁNJYÒU/yánjiū　　　FV/N: study; research
   研　　　　　　YÁN　　　　　　　　　research

	究	JYŌU/jīu	examine into
9.	道理	DÀULI/dàoli	N: teaching, doctrine
	理	LǏ	N: reason
10.	講	JYǍNG/jiǎng	FV: explain, talk, say
11.	好是好	HǍUSHRHǍU/haoshihao	PH: it is good all right..
12.	不過	BUGWÒ/buguò	A: but
13.	約會	YWĒHWÈI/yūehùi	N: appointment
	約	YWĒ/yuē	agreement
14.	算了吧	SWÀNLE BA/suànle ba	PH: forget it, drop it
15.	反正	FǍNJÈNG/fǎnzhèng	MA: in any case, anyway
	反	FǍN	the reverse side
16.	坐滿了	DZWÒMǍNLE/zùomǎnle	RV: all seats are taken
	滿	MǍN	SV: be full
17.	安靜	ĀNJING	SV: be quite, peaceful
	靜	JÌNG	quiet, peaceful
18.	dzwò位	DZWÒWEI/zuòwei	N: seat
19.	不久	BÙJYǑU/bùjiǔ	A: before long
20.	dzàn美shr	DZÀNMĚISHR̄/zànměishī	N: hymn
21.	跟着唱	GĒNJE CHÀNG/gēnzhe chàng	PH: to sing along
	跟着	GĒNJE/gēnzhe	CV: follow
22.	低頭	DĪTÓU	VO: to bow the head
	低	DĪ	SV/FV: be low/lower, bow
23.	chídǎu	qídǎu	FV: pray
24.	mùshr	mushi	N: pastor, minister
25.	講道	JYǍNGDÀU/jiǎngdào	VO: preach

26. 故事　　GÙSHR/gùshi　　N: story, tale

　　　故　　　GÙ　　　　　old, ancient

27. 窮得沒飯吃　CHYÚNGDE MÉIFÀN CHR̄/　PH: so poor that he was
　　　　　　　qióngde méifàn chī　　　without food to eat

　　　窮　　　CHYÚNG/qióng　　SV: be poor

23. 苦　　　KǓ　　　　SV: be hard up, in diffi-
　　　　　　　　　　　culties; bitter to the
　　　　　　　　　　　taste

29. 死　　　SŽ/sǐ　　　FV: die

30. 活　　　HWÓ/húo　　FV/SV: live/be alive

31. dyōu 了　　DYŌULE/diūle　　FV: lost

32. 地理　　DÌLǏ　　　N: geography

33. 對…有研究　DWÈI ... YǑU YÁNJYŌU/　PAT: be well versed in
　　　　　　　dùi ... yǒu yánjīu

34. 生活　　SHĒNGHWÓ/shēnghúo　N/FV: living/live

35. 不理　　BÙLǏ　　　FV: pay no attention to

36. 好像　　HǍUSYÀNG/hǎoxiàng MA: as though, it seems that

37. 約　　　YWĒ/yūe　　FV: to make an appointment

38. 反對　　FǍNDWÈI/fǎndùi　　FV: oppose

39. 過去了　GWÒCHYULE/gùoqule RV: passed away

40. 走過去　DZǑUGWOCHYÙ/zǒuguoqù RV: go (over) there

LESSON 8

Characters	Explanations	Expressions	
運 运	YÙN BF/V: luck; move around/ transport	運氣 運河	yùnchi N: luck, fortune N: canal
動 动	DÙNG dòng V: move	運動 運動會 自動	V/N: take physical exercise/ physical exercise N: athletic meeting A: automatically, voluntarily
場 场	CHĂNG BF: field	運動場 飛機場	N: athletic field N: air field
圖 图	TÚ N: picture, map, diagram	圖書館 地圖	N: library N: map
樹 树	SHÙ N: tree	大樹 樹木 樹皮	N: big tree N: trees N: bark

Characters	Explanations	Expressions
草	*TSĂU* N: grass, straw *căo*	草地 N: lawn
涼 凉 **alternate**	*LYÁNG* be cool, cold *liáng*	涼快 SV: be cool 着涼 jáulyáng VO: catch cold

休	*SYŌU* BF: rest
	xīu
		休息 N/V: rest
		休假 VO: close (school)
		      for a
		      vacation/to
		      have a
		      vacation

息	*SYĪ* BF: rest *xī*	休息 N/V: rest
種 种	*JŬNG* M: kind, species *zhŏng*	捸種 M: all sorts

Characters	Explanations	Expressions
鳥 鸟	*NYǍUR* N: bird *niǎo (r)*	鳥兒叫 singing of birds
課 课	*KÈ* M/N: (for lessons)/ school work	上課 VO: go to classes; class in session 下課 VO: class dismissed; to leave class 課堂 N: class room
參 参	*TSĀN* *cān* BF: participate in, collate, compare	參觀 V: pay a visit to (a public place), inspect inform- ally, go sight- seeing
觀 观	*GWĀN* BF: see, look at *guān*	參觀 V: pay a visit to (a public place), inspect informally, go sightseeing
省	*SHĚNG* N/V: province/save, economize	廣東省 PW: Kwangtung Province

Characters	Explanations	Expressions
假	*JYÀ* jìa N: vacation, leave of absence	放假 VO: close school for a vacation, to have a vacation 請假 VO: ask leave 春假 N: spring vacation
規 規	*GWĒI* gūi BF: custom, usage, regulation	規定 V: regulate
冷	*LĚNG* SV: be cold	冷水 N: cold water 冷笑 V/N: cold, heartless laugh; sarcastic grin
雪	*SYWĚ* xŭe N: snow	下雪 VO: snow (falls)
綠 绿	*LYÙ* lǜ SV: be green	草綠顏色 N: grass green color

第八課　故事

　　北海大學還有一個星期就要上課了。吃了午飯，張先生對小王說：

　　「今天我有事要到學校去，你願意跟我一塊兒去參觀參觀嗎？」

　　小王剛要說話，張小姐說：

　　「今天天氣很涼快，我們大家都去吧。」

　　張太太說：「我昨天夜裏着了點兒涼，我想在家裏休息休息。你們去吧。」

　　「好吧，」小王說，「我去開汽車去。」

　　張先生說：「學校離這兒不到一公里路，我們走着去吧。」

　　他們走了一會兒就到了北海大學了。

　　一進學校大門就是一條很長的路。路的兩邊兒有綠顏色的草地跟大樹。地方很大，收拾得也很乾淨。

　　小王說：「這個地方眞安靜，除了鳥兒叫以外，甚麼聲音都沒有。我眞沒想到，這兒夏天的風景這麼好。」

「夏天的風景還不算好。」張小姐說,「冬天下了雪這兒的風景就更好了, 那兒都是白的, 好看極了。」

「那一定很冷吧?」小王問。

「不冷, 一點兒也不冷。」張小姐說。

「你看見那個大樓沒有?」張先生問小王,「那就是學校的大禮堂。草地的那邊兒是 sùshè 我們學校規定, 從別省來的學生都得住校。你以後可以在那兒住。」

他們走了一會兒就到圖書館了。他們看見有很多學生在那兒念書。小王說:

「放假的時候怎麼還有學生來念書呢?」

張先生對張小姐說:「我還有別的事情。你帶國平到別的地方去看看吧。你們看完了先回家, 不用等我。」

張小姐帶着小王去看了 tǐyù 館跟運動場。張小姐問小王最喜歡那種運動。小王說:

「我在中學的時候每天念書, 不常運動。」

張小姐說:「運動很要緊。這兒有這麼大的運動場, 你以後應該常來。」

小王說:「當然, 當然。」

第八課　句子

1. 老李的信上常說，他們的學校有很大的運動場跟
   圖書館。

2. 他說他不常到運動場去，因爲他不太喜歡運動。

3. 可是他每天到圖書館去，因爲在那兒念書很安靜。

4. 圖書館的外頭有樹，有草地，所以夏天很涼快。

5. 他常常一個人在樹下頭休息，聽鳥兒叫。

6. 有的時候他們在圖書館上課，因爲圖書館比課堂[24]
   涼快。

7. 我很想去參觀參觀他們的學校，可是我不敢去，
   因爲我不會說國語。

8. 他說，不會說國語沒有關係，因爲他們的學校裏
   有很多從別省去的學生，他們的國語都說得不
   太好。

9. 他要我今年冬天，學校放假以後，去參觀。因爲
   學校規定，放假的時候學校可以讓人參觀。

10. 可是我聽說，北方的冬天很冷，常下雪，所以我[25]
    不敢去。

11. 老李說，今年秋天學校裏有一個運動會，所以放[26]
    三天假。

12.我給老李寫了一封航空信，告訴他，我決定坐十
　　月十二號下午一點零五分的特別快車到北jīng去。

13.我請他替我租一間屋子，因為我想在那兒休息一
　　個星期。

14.我到了北jīng，老李沒到車站來接我，我非常着急。

15.雖然是秋天，可是那天的天氣很冷，外頭下着雪。

16.我跟站上的人說:「我是剛從別省來的。請問，哪
　　兒有旅館？」

17.他說:「往東走，過一條街，有很多大樹，樹後頭
　　有一個草綠顏色的樓，那就是旅館。」

18.他說:「外頭下着雪呢，冷極了，你在這兒休息一
　　會兒吧。」

19.我給老李的學校打了一個電話。學校裏的人說，
　　老李上着課呢。他們學校規定，上課的時候學
　　生不可以接電話。

20.我在街上走了半天，可是沒看見草綠顏色的樓，
　　也沒看見甚麼大樹。

21.那個時候雪下得大極了。我覺得很冷，所以我在
　　一個鋪子裏買了一包烟，喝了一點兒熱茶。我
　　又買了一張北jīng地圖。

22.我打算立刻坐火車回南方³¹去，可是那個時候<u>老李</u>來了。

23.他說，他沒收到我的信。我說，大概是郵局送錯了。

24.我在<u>北 jīng</u>一共住了三天。每天都下雪，每天都很冷。我實在不喜歡那種天氣。

25.<u>老李</u>要我明年夏天再到<u>北 jīng</u>去，因為明年夏天他要畢業了。

26.他說，夏天<u>北 jīng</u>的風景好極了，ᵈ那兒都有樹，有綠的草地，ᵈ那兒都有鳥兒叫。

27.他要我在<u>上海</u>替他買一shwāng最新式的，草綠顏色的<u>德國</u>皮鞋。

28.他說:「這種皮鞋<u>北 jīng</u>買不着。你買了以後請立刻寄給我。價錢貴，不要緊。」

29.我在<u>上海</u>沒買着草綠顏色的皮鞋，所以我給他寄了一shwāng淺黃顏色的。

30.他來信說，我買的那shwāng皮鞋，大小很合適，可是他不喜歡那種顏色。

Vocabulary

New characters:

課　參　觀　涼　休
息　綠　草　樹　鳥
雪　冷　規　省　圖
假　運　動　場　種

---

1. 上課	SHÀNGKÈ	VO:	go to class
課	KÈ	M/N:	(for lessons)/school work
2. 參觀	TSĀNGWĀN/cānguān	FV:	pay a visit to, go sightseeing (to a public place
參	TSĀN/cān		participate in
觀	GWĀN/guān		see; look at
3. 涼快	LYÁNGKWÀI/liángkuài	SV:	be cool
涼	LYÁNG/liáng	SV:	be cool; cold
4. 着涼	JÁULYÁNG/zhāoliáng	VO:	catch cold
5. 休息	SYŌUSYI/xīusi	N/FV:	rest
休	SYŌU/xīu		rest
息	SYÍ/xí		rest
6. 綠	LYÙ/lǜ	SV:	be green
7. 草地	TSĂUDÌ/cǎodì	N:	grass, lawn
草	TSĂU/cǎo	N:	grass
8. 樹	SHÙ	N:	tree
9. 鳥兒叫	NYĂUR JYÀU/ niǎor jiào	PH:	the birds sing, singing of birds

	鳥	NYĂUR/niǎor	N: bird
10.	不算	BÚSWÀN/búsuàn	FV: cannot be considered
11.	下雪	SYÀSYWĔ/xiàxuĕ	VO: to snow
	雪	SYWĔ/xuĕ	N: snow
12.	冷	LĔNG	SV: be cold
13.	大禮堂	DÀLĬTÁNG	N: auditorium
14.	sùshè	SÙSHÈ	N: dormitory
15.	規定	GWĒIDÌNG/guīdìng	N/FV: regulation/regulate
	規	GWĒI/guī	custom, usage
16.	省	SHĔNG	N: province
17.	住校	JÙSYÀU/zhùxiào	VO: live at school
18.	圖書館	TÚSHŪGWĂN/túshūguǎn	N: library
	圖	TÚ	picture, map, diagram
19.	放假	FÀNGJYÀ/fàngjià	VO: to have a vacation
	假	JYÀ/jià	N: vacation, leave
20.	tǐyù館	TĬYUGWĂN/tǐyùguǎn	N: gym
21.	運動場	YÙNDÙNGCHĂNG/yùndòngchǎng	N: athletic field
	運	YÙN	FV: to ship
	動	DÙNG/dòng	FV: to move
	場	CHĂNG	field
22.	種	JŬNG/zhǒng	M: kind, species
23.	運動	YÙNDÙNG/yùndòng	N/FV: sports, physical exercise/to do physical exercise
24.	課堂	KÈTÁNG	N: classroom
25.	北方	BĔIFĀNG	PW: the north
26.	運動會	YÙNDÙNGHWÈI/yùndonghui	N: athletic meeting
27.	過(NuM)	GWÒ (Nu M jyē/ guò (Nu M jiē/	PH: go (Nu) blocks

28. 接電話 JYĒ DIÀNHWÀ/jiē diànhùa VO: *answer the phone*

29. 包 BĀU/bāo M: *pack (of cigarettes)*

30. 地圖 DÌTÚ N: *map*

31. 南方 NÁNFĀNG PW: *the south*

LESSON 9

Characters	Explanations	Expressions
歷 历	LÌ BF: pass through	經歷 V/N: experienced/ experience
史	SHŘ shǐ BF: history	歷史 N: history 歷史家 N: historian
總 总	DZǑNG zǒng A: always, in every case (interchangeable with 老)	總理 N: premier (of a republic)
擧 举	JYǓ jǔ V: raise	擧手 VO: raise one's hand 擧起來 RV: lift up 擧行 V: convene, hold (a meeting)
題 题	TÍ BF: theme, subject	問題 wèntí N: question, problem

Characters	Explanations	Expressions
連 连	*LYÁN* *lián* even, even including/join	連起來 RV: join together
答	*DÁ* V: answer, reply	回答 N/V: answer 答不出來 RV: unable to answer
練 练	*LYÀN* V: practice *liàn*	練車 VO: practice driving (an automobile) 練字 VO: practice handwriting
習 习	*SYÍ* BF: practice, learn *xí*	練習 lyànsyi N/V: practice 學習 N/V: study
俄	*È* BF: Russia	俄國 N: Russia

Characters	Explanations	Expressions
借	*JYÈ* V: borrow, lend *jìe*	借給 V: lend to 借錢 VO: borrow or lend money
英	*YĪNG* BF: England	英國 N: England 英文 N: English
交	*JYĀU* V: give to, deliver, communicate *jiāo*	交給 V: turn over to, hand over to 外交 N: diplomatic relations
利	*LÌ* BF: profit, advantage	利害 lìhai SV: be fierce, severe
害	*HÀI* BF: harm, disadvantage	利害 lìhai SV: be fierce, severe

Characters	Explanations	Expressions
何	*HÉ* BF: what? how? why? which?	何必 A: what need? why must? 何必非……不可 why insist on......
費 <small>费</small>	*FÈI* V/BF: waste, expend/ expenditure	費錢 VO/SV: cost money/ be expensive, wasteful 費時候 VO/SV: take time/ be time consuming 小費 N: tip, gratuity 學費 N: school tuition 郵費 N: postage
考	*KĂU* *kǎo* V: examine, test	考試 N: examinations 參考 V: compare, use for reference 參考書 N: a reference book
社 <small>社</small>	*SHÈ* BF: society, community	社會 N: society 社會學 N: sociology 旅行社 N: traveling agency
形	*SYÍNG* *xíng* figure, form, appearance (BF)	情形 chíngsying N: condition, situation 形容 V: describe

第九課　故事

　　北海大學開學了。那天早上小王跟小李很早就
到學校去了。小李對小王說:

　「我想念一門歷史，一門地理，一門俄文。」

　「你何必念俄文呢?」小王覺得很奇怪。

　「我在中學的時候覺得英文很難，考試的時候總
是考得不好，所以現在想試一試俄文。」

　　小王說:「不管你學英文hwò是俄文都得常常練
習，要是不練習，一定學不好。」

　　小李說:「那麼我們一塊兒學俄文，好不好?我
們可以常在一塊兒練習。我有甚麼問題可以問你，
你有甚麼問題也可以問我。這樣，我敢保險，我們
一定可以學得好。」

　　小王說:「我連英文都沒學好,怎麼能學俄文呢!
算了吧。」

　　小王看了一會兒gūng課表說:「我得念一門社
會學。」

　　小李說:「聽說教社會學的那位先生姓高叫思遠,
利害極了，考試的時候問題總是很難，我可不敢上

他的課。」

　　小王説:「可是高先生對社會學很有研究,他寫了很多有名的書。」

　　「我們念別的吧,何必非念社會學不可呢[20]?」小李説。

　　「過一會兒,高先生上課的時候,我們到他的課堂裏去聽聽。要是情形[21]不錯我們就念社會學,要是情形不好我們就不念。你説,成不成?」

　　小李想了一想説:「成,成。」

　　社會學在四十號課堂上課。他們到了那兒的時候,課堂裏已經有很多學生了。他們兩個人立刻找了一個dzwò位坐下。快到上課的時候,學生ywè 來ywè 多[22],把課堂都坐滿了。一會兒來了一位六七十歲的老先生。課堂裏立刻連一點兒聲音都沒有了。

小李問小王説:

　　「他就是高先生嗎?」

　　小王説:「大概是吧。」

　　高先生在黑bǎn[23] 上寫了二十多本參考書[24]的名字,要學生自己去看。小李舉手問高先生説:[25]

　　「那些書都得買嗎?」

「不必買。」高先生回答,「圖書館裏都有,你們可以去借。」

學生們問了很多社會學的問題。高先生回答得很清楚。學生們把他說的話都寫下來。一會兒下課了。小李問小王說:

「高先生怎麼不講書呢?」

小王說:「在大學裏念書,書都得自己去看,有甚麼問題,上課的時候大家研究。」

小李覺得這種念書的法子很有意思。那天晚上小李給他的朋友們寫了很多信,告訴他們,他現在正在研究社會學。他是高思遠先生的學生。他說在大學裏研究跟在中學裏念書的情形不一樣。他很高興,因為他現在是北海大學的學生了。

第九課　句　子

1. 我還記得<u>老高</u>，他上歷史課的時候總坐在我的左邊兒。

2. 他常常舉手問問題，有的時候他的問題很奇怪，連先生都不能回答。

3. 要是先生問我們一個問題，他總是第一個舉手，雖然他不一定會回答。

4. 他也學俄文，他說，學俄文得常練習。

5. 有的時候他用俄文問我一個問題，我沒用俄文回答，他就不高興。

6. 他常常借我的歷史書去看。他說，他很窮，買不起書。

7. 他說，他父母活着的時候很有錢，家裏有很多金的跟銀的東西。

8. 可是他十歲的時候父母都死了，所以他ywè 來 ywè 窮了。

9. 有一個冬天的夜裏，他家來了一個賊，把值錢的東西都偷走了。

10. 警察局雖然派了很多警察去找那個賊，可是沒找

着。

11.後來他苦極了，苦得連飯都吃不起。

12.現在他白天在一個公司裏賣布，晚上到學校裏來
　　念書。

13.我問他結婚了沒有。他說，他連飯都吃不起，那
　　兒有錢結婚。

14.有一天老高到我家來，對我說，他需要六十塊錢。
　　他問我能不能暫時借給他。

15.他說他沒有錢給房租。房東太太很利害。要是他
　　不給錢就不能在那兒住。

16.我說我得到銀行去取。我約他明天到我家來取錢。

17.第二天老高來了。我交給他七十塊錢。我說:「另
　　外的十塊錢給你買皮鞋。你的那shwāng 皮鞋應
　　該換了。」

18.老高說:「皮鞋太貴，我去買一shwāng布鞋吧。反
　　正布鞋也很結實，何必非買皮鞋不可呢！」

19.春假的時候我想約老高到鄉下去休息幾天。他說:
　　「旅行又費錢又費時候，我不去。」

20.我在鄉下病了，病得很利害。我真希望有朋友來
　　看看我。

21.老高聽說我病了，就來看我。他是坐飛機來的。

22.我問他，買飛機票的錢是誰給他的。他說他是跟他的公司借的。

23.春假以後我很久沒看見老高。上歷史課的時候他也沒去。

24.有一天晚上我到他家去。他屋子裏的燈沒開。我想他一定沒在家。我在屋子外頭等了一會兒就走了。

25.我回家的時候看見牆上有一封信。

26.我一看就知道是老高寫的。他說他沒有錢，所以不能再念書了。

27.他說，這個世界上不念書的人反正也可以生活，何必非念書不可。

28.他說，他有一個朋友介紹他到廣東省去作事。他已經決定走了。

29.老高走了。我們上歷史課的時候沒有人再舉手問問題。

30.有一天我剛考完社會學，我收到老高的一封很簡單的信。信上說，他那兒的情形很好。

Vocabulary

New characters:

歷　史　俄　何　英
考　練　習　題　連
社　利　害　總　形
舉　答　借　交　費

---

1. 開學	KĀISYWÉ/kāixué	VO:	school starts
2. 門	MÉN	M:	(for courses)
3. 歷史	LÌSHR/lìshǐ	N:	history
歷	LÌ		pass through
史	SHR/shǐ		history
4. 地理	DÌLǏ	N:	geography
5. 俄文	ÈWÉN	N:	Russian language
俄	È		Russia
6. 何必	HÉBÌ	A:	what need is there?, why insist on ?
何	HÉ		what? how? why?
7. 英文	YĪNGWÉN	N:	English language
英	YĪNG		England
8. 考試	KǍUSHR/kǎoshì	FV/N:	examine, test/exam
考	KǍU/kǎo	FV:	examine, test
9. hwò 是	HWÒSHR/huòshì	A:	or
10. 練習	LYÀNSYÍ/liànxí	FV/N:	practice/practice; exercise

	練	LYÀN/liàn	FV: practice
	習	SYÍ/xí	practice, learn
11.	那麼	NÈMMA	A: in that case
12.	問題	WÈNTÍ	N: question, problem, theme
	題	TÍ	theme, subject
13.	我敢保險	WǑ GǍN BǍUSYǍN/wǒ gǎn bǎoxiǎn	PH: I can be sure that
14.	連····都····	LYÁN ... DŌU/lián...dōu	PAT: even ...
	連	LYÁN/lián	CV: even
15.	gūng課表	GŪNGKÈBYÁU/gōngkèbiǎo	N: schedule of classes
16.	社會學	SHÈHWÈISYWÉ/shèhuìxué	N: sociology
	社	SHÈ	society
17.	利害	LÌHAI	SV: be fierce; severe, strict
	利	LÌ	profit, advantage
	害	HÀI	harm, disadvantage
18.	總(是)	DZǓNG (SHR)/zǒng(shi)	A: always
19.	可	KĚ	A: indeed
20.	何必非... 不可	HÉBÌ FĒI ... BÙKĚ	PAT: why insist on ...
21.	情形	CHÍNGSYING/qíngxing	N: situation, condition(s)
	形	SYÍNG/xíng	figure; form
22.	ywè來ywèSV	YWÈLÁIYWÈ/yùeláiyùe	PAT: getting SV-er and SV-er
23	黑 bǎn	HĒIBǍN	N: blackboard
24.	參考書	TSĀNKǍUSHŪ/cānkǎoshū	N: reference book
25.	舉手	JYǓSHǑU /júshǒu	VO: raise hand
	舉	JYǓ/jǔ	raise
26.	回答	HWÉIDÁ/huídá	FV: answer
	答	DÁ	FV: answer
27.	借	JYÈ/jìe	FV: borrow; lend

28.	講書	JYǍNGSHŪ/jiǎngshū	VO: explain the lesson
29.	交給	JYĀUGĚI/jiāogěi	FV: turn over to, hand
	交	JYĀU/jiāo	give to; deliver
30.	春假	CHWŪNJYÀ/chūnjìa	N: Spring vacation
31.	費錢	FÈICHYÁN/fèiqián	VO/SV: cost money; waste money/be expensive
	費	FÈI	FV: use a lot of; waste
32.	廣東省	GWǍNGDŪNGSHĚNG/ guǎngdōngshěng	PW: Kwangtung Province Guangdong Province

LESSON 10

Characters	Explanations	Expressions
痛	TÙNG SV: be painful tòng	頭痛 SV: have a headache
發 发	FĀ BF: put forth, start, send, become, grow, develop	發明 N/V: invention/ invent 發現 V/N: discover/ discovery
燒 烧	SHĀU V: burn shāo	發燒 VO: have a fever
原	YWÁN BF: origin, reason, cause yuán	原來 MA: originally 原故 N: reason, cause
私	SZ̄ BF: private sī	私立 BF: privately established (such as school) 自私 SV: selfish

Characters	Explanations	Expressions	
醫 医	YĪ BF: heal, cure; a doctor	醫生 中醫 西醫	N: a doctor N: Chinese doctor (trained to practice Chinese medicine) N: Western doctor (trained to practice Western medicine)
院	YWÀN BF: courtyard, hall; yuàn institution	醫院 院子	N: hospital, dispensary N: the yard, court
科	KĒ N/BF: department/science	外科 科學 科學家	N: surgical department N/SV: science/be scientific N: scientist
護 护	HÙ BF: protect, guard	護航 看護 保護	V: convoy N/V: a nurse/nurse V/N: protect/ protection
士	SHR̀ BF: professional person shì (orig. scholar, warrior)	護士	N: nurse

Characters	Explanations	Expressions
檢 检	JYĂN jiǎn BF: examine	檢查 BF: examine
查	CHÁ V: investigate, inspect, look up	檢查 V: examine 查病 VO: be examined for a disease
溫	WĒN BF: be warm; review (lessons)	溫水 N: warm water
度	DÙ M: degree	溫度 N: temperature 十五度 NU-M: fifteen degrees 溫度表 N: thermometer
藥 药	YÀU yào N: medicine, drug, herb	吃藥 VO: take medicine 藥房 N: drug store, dispensary

Characters	Explanations	Expressions

照	JÀU
	zhào V: reflect,
	         look after
		照像 VO: take
		            photographs
		照像機 N: camera

光	GWĀNG N: light, ray guāng	ㄨ光 N: X-ray 照ㄨ光 VO: take an X-ray picture

隨 随	SWÉI BF: follow
	suí
		隨便 A/SV: do as one
		           pleases/
		           be casual,
		           unconcerned
		隨時 A: at all times,
		           at any moment

味	WÈI BF: flavor, taste,
	        smell
		味兒 wèr
		       N: taste, odor,
		         aroma
		味道 wèidau
		       N: taste, odor,
		         aroma

雨	YǓ N: rain	下雨 VO: rain (falls)

第十課　故　事

　　有一個星期六的晚上，<u>小王</u>請<u>張</u>小姐到一個飯館兒去吃飯。那個飯館兒在<u>北jīng</u>城外頭。飯館兒的前頭有草地，有樹，風景非常好，也非常安靜。飯館兒裏頭也收拾得很乾淨。<u>小王</u>跟<u>張</u>小姐說：

　　「這個飯館兒作的菜味¹兒很特別，所以我請你來試試。」

　　<u>小王</u>跟<u>張</u>小姐一邊²兒吃飯一邊兒談話。<u>小王</u>吃了很多。回家的時候，街上的風很大，又下了一點兒雨³。<u>小王</u>恐怕<u>張</u>小姐着凉⁴，所以把自己的大衣借給<u>張</u>小姐。回學校以後，就覺得有一點兒頭痛⁵。<u>小王</u>想，這大概是着了點兒凉，不要緊。第二天早上，<u>小王</u>覺得有點兒發燒⁶。因爲那天有考試，所以不能在家休息。到了晚上，病就更利害了。他的túng學⁷<u>小李</u>，就立刻把他送⁸到一個私立醫院⁹裏去。

　　醫院裏的<u>高</u>醫生¹⁰給<u>小王</u>檢查¹¹了一次，試了試溫度¹²，問了<u>小王</u>很多問題。<u>高</u>醫生說：

　　「這是因爲你吃了太多東西，又着了凉的原故¹³。」

　　醫生讓護士¹⁴給<u>小王</u>吃了一點兒藥¹⁵。護士對<u>小王</u>

說:

「你吃了這個藥，睡一夜，就好了。」

張小姐聽說小王病了，很着急，就到醫院裏去看他。張小姐問小王，「是甚麼病？醫生說要緊不要緊？吃了些甚麼藥？照了 X 光[16]沒有？」

小王說:「沒有甚麼病，就着了點兒涼。昨天晚上護士給我吃了點兒藥，今天就好多了。」

張小姐說:「我父親去年也有過這樣的病，後來休息了一個星期就好了。這都是因爲你平常念書太用gūng[17]，不常運動，吃東西又太隨便[18]，所以病了。你應當好好兒[19]的休息休息。」

小王在醫院裏住了兩天，覺得好了。高醫生又給他檢查了一次。高醫生說:

「你今天可以回學校去了。可是你回去以後，吃東西還得小心。」

小王謝了高醫生，跟護士說了再見，就回學校去了。

第十課　句子

1. 去年夏天，我常常頭痛，發燒，不知道是甚麼原故。

2. 後來我到一個私立醫院去查病[20]，那個醫院離這兒就有三公里。

3. 醫院裏的人問我，是nèi[21]科是外科[22]。我說，我不知道。

4. 我告訴他，我頭痛，發燒。那個人要我到二樓去。

5. 我在二樓等了半天。有一個護士跟我說，該我了[23]。

6. 那位醫生姓李。李醫生給我檢查了半天，又給我試了試溫度。

7. 醫生說，我的溫度不高，沒甚麼病。他給了我一包藥。

8. 我不知道是甚麼藥，是深紅的，有一點兒像紅銅[24]的顏色。

9. 我要他給我照一張X光。他說，我不用照X光。

10. 他說，我吃了這包藥就不頭痛，不發燒了。

11. 我把那包藥吃了，可是還覺得頭痛，發燒。

12. 醫生又試了試我的溫度，問了我很多問題。

13. 他問我在哪兒作事？chōu烟不chōu烟？

14.我說，我在一個私立中學念書。平常一天大概chōu
一包烟，忙的時候一天chōu一包半。

15.吃飯的時候，不管吃甚麼東西都覺得沒有味兒。

16.醫生要我暫時在醫院裏留幾天。他要給我好好兒
的檢查檢查。

17.醫院裏的風景很好，有很多樹。我最喜歡一個人
坐在樹底下聽鳥兒叫。

18.可是那幾天每天都下雨，所以我除了吃飯以外就
給朋友寫信。

19.我在醫院住了三天，一共寫了二十封航空信。

20.每天中午我請一位護士替我到郵局寄信去。

21.我隨時都想回去，可是護士說，他們醫院規定，
病人不可以隨便出去。

22.我跟護士說，我在一個私立中學念書。那個私立
中學的gūng課特別忙。

23.後來醫生來了，醫生說，我的病是因爲念書太用
gūng的原故。

24.他說，這是一種新發現的病。現在科學家正在研
究，還沒有發明甚麼新藥。

25.他要我回去以後常常到運動場去運動，隨時出去

照照像,³¹ 玩兒玩兒。

26.我說,我秋天就要畢業了,畢業以前我一定常常
　　到學校的運動場去運動。

27.醫生說,要是我覺得頭痛,發燒,可以隨時去看
　　他。

28.我回家以後常常運動,沒有事的時候就開着汽車
　　出去玩兒。

29.那年秋天的畢業考試,我考得不太好,可是我覺
　　得很值得。³²

30.因為我回家以後一直的沒病過,³³ 不管吃甚麼東西
　　都覺得味兒不錯。

Vocabulary

New characters:

味　雨　痛　發　燒
私　醫　院　檢　查
溫　度　原　護　士
藥　照　光　隨　科

---

1. 味兒　　　WER　　　N: taste; odor; aroma
   味　　　　WEI　　　　　flavor, taste, smell

2. 一邊兒…　YIBYAR … YIBYAR　PAT: on one hand …
   一邊兒　　yìbiār … yìbiār　on the other hand …

3. 風　　　　FĒNG　　　N: wind

4. 下雨　　　SYÀYǓ　　　VO: rain (falls)
   　　　　　xìayǔ
   雨　　　　yǔ　　　　N: rain

5. 頭痛　　　TÓUTÙNG　　SV: have a headache
   　　　　　tóutòng
   痛　　　　TÙNG tòng　SV: be painful

6. 發燒　　　FĀSHĀU/fāshāo VO: have a fever
   發　　　　FĀ　　　　put forth; start; grow
   燒　　　　SHĀU/shāo　FV: burn

7. túng學　　TÚNGSYWÉ/tóngxué N: schoolmate

8. 私立　　　SZLÌ/sīlì　AT: privately established
   　　　　　　　　　　(such as a school)
   私　　　　SZ/ sī　　private

9. 醫院　　　YĪYWÀN/yīyuàn N: hospital, dispensary

醫	YĪ	cure; doctor
院	YWÀN/yuàn	courtyard; hall; institution

10. 醫生 YĪSHENG   N: doctor

11. 檢查 JYǍNCHÁ/jiǎnchá FV: examine; look into

    檢 JYǍN/jiǎn   examine

    查 CHÁ   FV: investigate

12. 溫度 WĒNDÙ   N: temperature

    溫 WĒN   SV: be warm

    度 DÙ   M: degree

13. 原故 YWÁNGÙ/yuángù N: reason, cause

    原 YWÁN/yuán   origin; cause; reasons

14. 護士 HÙSHR/hùshi   N: nurse

    護 HÙ   protect, guard

    士 SHR̀/shì   professional person; scholar

15. 藥 YÀU/yào   N: medicine, drug; herb

16. 照 X 光 JÀU AÌKESZGWĀNG   VO: take an X-ray picture
    zhào aīkesiguāng
    照 JÀU/zhào   FV: reflect
    光 GWĀNG/guāng   N: light, ray

17. 用 gūng YÙNGGŪNG/yònggōng SV: study hard

18. 隨便 SWÉIBYÀN/súibiàn A/SV: do as one pleases/be casual; unconcerned

    隨 SWÉI/súi   follow

19. 好好兒的 HǍUHǍURDE/hǎohǎorde A: nicely, carefully

20. 查病 CHÁBÌNG   VO: be examined for a disease

21. nèi科 NÈIKĒ   N: internal medicine department

    科 KĒ   department

22. 外科 WÀIKĒ   N: surgical department

23. 該我了   *GĀI WǑ LE*   *PH: Now it is my turn.*

24. 紅銅   *HÚNGTÚNG/hóngtóng N: copper*

25. 隨時   *SWÉISHŔ/suíshí   A: at all times; at any time*

26. 病人   *BÌNGRÉN   N: patient, sick person*

27. gūng課   *GŪNGKÈ/gōngke   N: school work, homework*

28. 發現   *FĀSYÀN/fāxiàn   FV: discover*

29. 科學家   *KĒSYWÉJYĀ/kēxuéjiā N: scientist*

    科學   *KĒSYWÉ/kēxué   N: science*

    …家   *... JYĀ/jiā   BF: suffix indicating a specialist*

30. 發明   *FĀMÍNG   FV: invent*

31. 照照像   *JÀUJÀUSYÀNG/zhàozhàoxiàng FV: take photos*
            NOTE: reduplication of functive verbs indicates casualness

    照像   *JÀUSYÀNG/zhàoxiàng VO: take photographs*

32. 值得   *JŔDE/zhíde   SV: be worthwhile*

33. 一直沒…過 *YÌJŔ MÉI V GWÒ   PAT: never (verbed)*
            yìzhí méi V guò

LESSON 11

Characters	Explanations	Expressions
身	SHĒN BF: the body,	動身　VO: start (on a trip)
體 体	TĬ　BF: the body	身體　N: the body 檢查身體 VO: have a physical examination
精	JĪNG BF: spirit, essence	精明　SV: shrewd 酒精　N: alcohol
神 神	SHÉN BF: spirit [N: deity, God]	精神　N: spirit, the spiritual part of man 有精神 SV: full of spirit and energy
同	TÚNG BF: be the same tóng	同學　VO/N: attend the same school/ schoolmate 同事　VO/N: work at the same kind of work/ colleague 同鄉　N: fellow townsman 同意　V: agree

123

124   Read Chinese II

Characters	Explanations	Expressions
湖	*HÚ* N: lake	湖南 PW: Hunan Province 湖北 PW: Hupeh Province
花	*HŪA (R)* flower *hūa (r)*	花木 N: flowers and trees, vegetation 花房 • N: greenhouse
石	*SHŔ* BF: stone, rock *shí*	石頭 shŕtou N: stone, rock
處	*CHÙ* BF: place, office, point, feature	處處 N: everywhere 好處 N: good point, benefit 壞處 N: bad point 到處 N: everywhere
如	*RÚ* BF: be like, as, if	不如 V: be not as good as

Characters	Explanations	Expressions
而	*ER* BF: but, while on the other hand, and, and yet	而且 A: besides, moreover, in addition
且	*CHYĚ* BF: moreover, furthermore qǐe	而且 A: besides, moreover, in addition
只	*JR* A: just, only zhǐ	只是 A: just, only 只好 A: the best thing is to.....
既 既	*JÌ* MA: since, inasmuch as	既然 MA: since (it is so)
球	*CHYÓU* N: ball qíu	打球 VO: play ball 看打球 Ph: go to a ball game

Characters	Explanations	Expressions
影	*YǏNG* BF: shadow, image, reflection	電影 N: motion picture 電影院 N: movie theater
戲 戏	*SYÌ* N: play, opera xì	聽戲 VO: go to a play 看戲 VO: go to a play
陽 阳	*YÁNG* BF: male principle in nature	太陽 tàiyang N: the sun 陽光 N: sun light
並 并	*BÌNG* BF/P: and, also, at the same time/ intensive particle before negatives	並且 MA: moreover (interchangeable with 而且
園 园	*YWÁN* BF: garden, park yuán	公園 N: park 花園 N: flower garden

第十一課　故　事

　　有一個星期六，小李到小王的屋子裏來問小王：
「城裏那個德國電影[1]你看了沒有？」

「我不知道有甚麼德國電影。」小王說。

「報上那麼大的廣告你沒看見嗎？我剛才跟幾個
朋友去看了，好極了，看的人眞多，那麼大的一個
電影院[2]都坐滿了。」

　　「眞的嗎？」小王很高興的說，「今天下午我反正
要約張小姐出去玩兒，我就請他去看電影吧。」

　　小王在電影院裏買了兩張票，就立刻到張家去
跟張小姐說：

「今天城裏那個德國電影很不錯，我剛才買了兩
張票，我們快一點兒走吧。」

　　「看電影有甚麼意思！」張小姐說，「今天太陽[3]這
麼好，我們不如[4]到北海公園[5]去玩兒玩兒。」

　　小王說：「可是我已經買了票了。而且今天那個
電影好極[6]了。學校裏有很多同學[7]去看了，都說好。」

　　「你總想看電影是甚麼原故？」張小姐很不高興
的說，「你看太陽那麼好，爲甚麼不到公園裏去玩兒

呢？並且你念了一個星期的書，天天在課堂裏，連一點兒運動也沒有。星期六到外頭去走走，對你的身體，精神都有好處。」

「可是……」

「你大概還沒到北海公園去過吧？」張小姐接着說，「那兒的風景好極了，到處都有紅的花，綠的樹，還有很多石頭。特別在湖邊兒上，安靜極了。」

小王說:「上禮拜我要去聽戲，後來你決定去打球。上次是你決定的，這次應該讓我決定。今天那個電影我非看不可。」

張小姐聽了這個話很生氣的說:

「我原來就沒想出去。你既然覺得這個電影非看不可，你一個人去吧。我不去。」

張太太看了這個情形，很同情小王，就跟他們兩個人說:

「你們兩個人今天去看電影，明天到公園去，怎麼樣？」

「今天的太陽這麼好，我不去看電影。」張小姐還不同意，「誰敢說明天還有這麼好的天氣？要不然就今天到公園去，明天去看電影。」

<u>小王</u>沒法子，只好²²說:「好，就這麼辦吧。」

第十一課　句子

1. 一九六〇年的夏天，我母親死了。那個時候我的
   身體跟精神都非常壞。

2. 有一天我的同學黃子安來看我。他一看見我就說:
   「你的身體跟精神怎麼這麼壞呢！」

3. 他說，他家在鄉下，那兒的風景很好，有湖，有
   樹，有花兒；還有好看的石頭。

4. 他說:「你需要休息，要是你同意到我家去住，對
   你的身體跟精神一定有好處。」

5. 我原來不想去。我想在同學家住不如在自己家住。

6. 而且我家的花園子不錯。雖然沒有湖，可是到處
   都有花兒，到處都有石頭，何必非到鄉下去不
   可呢。

7. 可是子安很熱心，一定要我去，所以我只好說:
   「你既然一定要我去，我就去住一個星期吧。」

8. 那是我第一次看見子安的姐姐，子英，那天他穿
   了一件深綠顏色的布衣shang。

9. 他的那shwāng　淺黃的皮鞋雖然樣子不太新，可
   是很合適。

10.子安給我們介紹了以後，子英小姐就對我說:「我已經給nín 收拾了一間屋子，nín 要洗洗臉，換換衣shang 嗎?」

11.我們不久就成了很好的朋友。他聽說我是研究社會學的，所以常常問我社會學的問題。

12.他的問題雖然很簡單，可是我總覺得我回答得不夠清楚。

13.子英的國語雖然說得不太好，可是他會說德文也會說俄文，他常要跟我練習說德文。

14.可是我的德文說得不如他，所以我只好說，我不會說。

15.我們常一塊兒在湖邊兒上打球，坐在石頭上談話。

16.有的時候我們談歷史，地理;有的時候我們也談看電影跟聽戲。

17.鄉下的天氣好極了，差不多每天都有太陽，從來不下雨，並且也不太熱。

18.我在鄉下住了三個月，差不多天天打球，我的身體比以前結實多了，作事情也有精神了。

19.有一天我接着從廣東省寄來的一封航空信，那封信是我從前的一個同事寫的。

20.他說，他在廣東省有一個保險公司，希望我能去
　　參觀，而且希望我能幫他作一點兒事。

21.我動身的那一天，子安跟子英送我到飛機場去。
　　子英說再見的時候，聲音很低，好像快哭了。

22.我總覺得廣東那個地方不如北平。那兒的花兒不
　　如北jīng的好看；那兒的石頭不如北jīng的奇怪；
　　那兒的湖也不如北jīng的有意思。

23.雖然我常去聽戲，打球，可是我的精神ywè來ywè
　　壞。我覺得在那兒作事對我沒有好處；我覺得
　　苦極了。

24.可是我既然來了當然不能隨便走，所以我跟那個
　　同事商量，告訴他，我想回北jīng去。

25.那個同事很同情我。他說:「沒有關係，你回去吧。」

26.一九六一年的冬天，我給黃家打了一個電報，告
　　訴他們，我坐十二月四號早上八點零五分的飛
　　機回北jīng。

27.我下飛機的時候就看見子安一個人來接我。他說，
　　子英今年春天已經結婚了，而且快有孩子了。

28.我既然到了北jīng，當然應該去看看子英，可是子
　　安不同意。他說，子英這兩天身體不好，最好

不去看他。

29.我在黃家住了兩天。我覺得湖邊兒上不如以前好
玩兒；石頭也不如以前好看；連太陽都不如以
前。

30.我覺得世界上甚麼東西都沒有意思；我也不知道
爲甚麼我還活在這個沒有意思的世界上。

Vocabulary

New characters

影　陽　如　園　而
且　同　並　身　體
精　神　處　花　石
湖　戲　球　旣　只

----

1. 電影　　DYÀNYǏNG/diànyǐng N: motion picture, movie
   影　　　YǏNG　　　　　　　shadow; image
2. 電影院　DYÀNYǏNGYWÀN/diànyǐngyuàn N: movie theatre
3. 太陽　　TÀIYANG　　　　N: sun
   陽　　　YÁNG　　　　　　sun
4. 不如　　BÙRÚ　　　　　FV: be not as good as
   如　　　RÚ　　　　　　　be like
5. 公園　　GŪNGYWÁN/gōngyuán N: park
   園　　　YWÁN/yuán　　　　　garden; park
6. 而且　　ÉRCHYĚ/érqiě　　MA: moreover, besides
   而　　　ÉR　　　　　　　but; and
   且　　　CHYĚ/qiě　　　　　moreover
7. 同學　　TÚNGSYWÉ/tóngxué N: schoolmate, classmate
   同　　　TÚNG/tóng　　　　be the same
8. 並且　　BÌNGCHYĚ/bìngqiě MA: moreover
   並　　　BÌNG　　　　　　and; also

9. 身體   SHĒNTĬ   N: health; body
    身   SHĒN   body
    體   TĬ   body

10. 精神   JĪNGSHEN   N: spirit
    精   JĪNG   spirit, essence
    神   SHÉN   spirit, deity, god

11. 好處   HĂUCHÙ/hǎochù   N: good point, benefit
    處   CHÙ   BF: point, place

12. 到處   DÀUCHÙ/dàochù   N: everywhere

13. 花   HWĀ/huā   N: flower

14. 石頭   SHŔTOU/shítou   N: rock, stone
    石   SHŔ/shí   rock, stone

15. 湖邊兒 HÚBYĀR/húbiār   PW: lake shore, lake side
    湖   HÚ   N: lake

16. 聽戲   TĪNGSYÌ/tīngxì   VO: go to a play
    戲   SYÌ/xì   N: play, (Chinese) opera

17. 打球   DĂCHYÓU/dǎqiú   VO: play ball
    球   CHYÓU/qiú   N: ball

18. 原來   YWÁNLÁI/yuánlái   MA: originally, in the first place

19. 旣然   JÌRÁN   MA: since
    旣   JÌ   since

20. 同情   TÚNGCHÍNG/tóngqíng   FV: be sympathetic with

21. 同意   TÚNGYÌ/tóngyì   FV: agree with

22. 只好   JŔHĂU/zhíhǎo   A: the best thing to do is
    只   JŔ/zhǐ   only, just

23. 花園子 HWĀYWÁNDZ/huāyuánzi   N: flower garden

24. 成   CHÉNG   FV: become

25. 同事   TÚNGSHR̀/tóngshì   N: co-worker

26. 動身   DÙNGSHĒN/dòngshēn   VO: start (on a trip)

27. 飛機塲   FĒIJĪCHǍNG   N: airport

LESSON 12

Characters	Explanations		Expressions	
青	$CH\bar{I}NG$ $q\bar{i}ng$	be green, blue, black	年青 青年	SV: be young N: young person
鬧 闹	$N\grave{A}U$ $n\grave{a}o$	/SV: make disturbance/ be noisy	熱鬧 鬧鐘	rènau SV/N: be bustling, lively/ excitement N: alarm clock
尺	CHR $chǐ$	M/N: (a Chinese foot divided into ten inches roughly equivalent to fourteen English inches)/a foot rule	六尺高 三尺布	six feet tall three feet of cotton cloth
普	$PǓ$	BF: general, universal	普通	SV: be general, common
通	$TǓNG$ $t\bar{o}ng$	/V: all, universal/ go through; be reached by; communicate	普通 交通 通電話	SV: be general, common N: communications VO: make a phone call

137

Characters	Explanations	Expressions
誠 诚	*CHÉNG*　honest, sincere	誠實　SV: be honest, sincere
相	*SYĀNG*　mutual, reciprocal *xiāng*	相當　A: fairly, relatively 相信　V: believe
力	*LÌ*　BF: strength, power	用力　A: hard (make an effort) 力量　lìlyang N: strength
推	*TWĒI*　V: push *tuī*	推出去　RV: push out
拉	*LĀ*　V: pull	拉上來　RV: pull up

Characters	Explanations	Expressions
雞 鸡	JĪ N: chicken	公雞 N: cock 母雞 N: hen
蛋	DÀN N: egg	雞蛋 N: egg
肉	RÒU N: meat, flesh	雞肉 N: chicken meat
隻 只	JR̄ zhī M: (measure for animal, birds, etc.)	一隻雞 N: one chicken 兩隻船 N: two boats
主	JŬ zhǔ BF: master, host; main, chief	主意 júyi N: idea, plan 主人 N: master, host 主張 V: advocate; of opinion that, to hold (the opinion)

Characters	Explanations	Expressions
懒 懒	*LǍN* SV: be lazy	懒得利害 Ph: terribly lazy
趣	*CHYÙU* BF: interest qù	有趣 SV: be interesting 有興趣 SV/VO: be interested in, show interest in 趣味 chyùwei N: interest
惜	*SYĪ* BF: pity xī	可惜 MA/SV: too bad! unfortunately! what a pity!/be pitiful, pitiable, regrettable
忽	*HŪ* BF: suddenly, unexpectedly	忽然 MA: suddenly, unexpectedly
重	*JÙNG* SV: be heavy, important zhòng	重要 jùngyau SV: be important

第十二課　故事

　　星期日早上張小姐給小王打了一個電話說:

「我母親剛才買了一隻雞，一打雞蛋跟很多肉。今天晚上我請了幾位對社會問題有興趣的年青朋友來吃飯，我想一定相當熱鬧。要是你沒有別的重要的事情，請你也來吧。」

　　小王說:「我沒有甚麼重要的事情，不過小李今天約我一塊兒去dyàu魚。我大概六點鐘到你家，成不成?」

　　「那麼請小李也來吧。」張小姐說,「Òu！可別忘了送幾條魚給我們a！」

　　小王跟小李在河邊兒上dyàu了一天的魚，可是一條也沒dyàu着。小王說:

　　「怎麼辦，要是今天dyàu不着魚，張小姐一定要笑話我們。」

　　小李想了一想說:「別着急，我有了主意了，我們到鋪子裏去買幾條送給他們就成了。反正他們不會知道。」

　　小王說:「好主意，好主意。」

他們兩個人在鋪子裏買了五條大魚，就到張家
去了。

那個時候張家的客人很多，並且都是些年青人，
所以很熱鬧。大家看見了這麼大的魚很高興，就問
小王跟小李是怎麼dyàu着的。小李說：

「Dyàu魚的時候，最要緊的是安靜，不着急。一
着急就不成。比方說，今天下午我們在河邊兒上dyàu
魚。那條河裏的魚最難dyàu，普通人不容易dyàu着。
我在河邊兒上等了一會兒，覺得有一條魚來了，我
用力往上一拉，魚從水裏出來了，是一條青顏色的，
又重又大，差不多有二尺多長。沒想到小王一高興，
忽然一推我，那條魚一動，又dyàu下去了。你們說
可惜不可惜。後來我教他應該怎麼dyàu魚，不到兩
個鐘頭我們就dyàu着了五條。」

張小姐聽了不說話，只是笑。小李說：

「你不信可以問小王。」

「小王，」張小姐說，「我知道你很誠實。你說是真
的嗎？」

小王只是笑，不說話。張小姐說：

「你不說，我早就知道了。你們買錯魚了。這些

都是海魚。北jīng的河裏怎麼會有海魚呢？」

　小王跟小李都覺得不好意思。[26]

第十二課　句子

1. 我還記得我年青的時候，在一個私立大學念書的情形。

2. 老何，小張跟我三個人住在一塊兒，很熱鬧。

3. 老何有六尺多高，比普通人高半尺。小張只有五尺高。他們兩個人都很誠實。

4. 我們的房子在鄉下，房租按月算，每月六十塊錢，管燈，水。

5. 我們那兒離學校有十里路。每天早上我們得開汽車去上課。

6. 多天相當冷，而且常下雪，我們的汽車常常停在路上壞了。

7. 老何在後頭用力推，小張在前頭用力拉。

8. 我們都想換一lyàng²⁷ 新汽車，可惜我們都很窮，買不起。

9. 我們每個人，每天就吃三個雞蛋，三天吃一次肉。

10. 我們都喜歡吃雞，可是雞的價錢太貴，每隻賣一塊半錢。

11. 我覺得有汽車很費錢，所以主張把車賣了。²⁸ 可是

鄉下的交通²⁹不方便，沒有汽車不成。

12. 後來<u>老何</u>出了一個主意，³⁰他主張我們下了課去作一點兒事。

13. <u>老何</u>在一個旅館裏找着了事，<u>小張</u>在圖書館裏找着了事。我很懶，³¹所以一直³²找不着事。

14. 他們說我太懶，不讓我吃肉。我很着急，因爲我最愛吃肉。

15. 後來我在郵局裏找着了事。我每天晚上把郵局的屋子收拾乾淨。

16. 我對那個事情沒有甚麼興趣，並且學校的gūng課也相當忙，所以不久我又不作事了。

17. <u>老何</u>說，我是一個誠實的青年，³³可惜太懶。

18. 我說，我不是懶，我的身體不好，我得常吃肉跟雞蛋。

19. 有一天我在圖書館念書，忽然接着<u>老何</u>打來的一個電話。

20. 他說：「<u>小張</u>忽然頭痛，發燒了。剛才醫生給他檢查了一次，說他的病很普通，可是需要吃肉跟雞。」

21. <u>老何</u>問我，有沒有錢買雞。我說，我連買雞蛋的

錢都沒有。

22.我跟一個朋友借了十塊錢，買了一隻很重的雞，
　　一打雞蛋，另外又買了一點兒藥。

23.我正在給小張預備飯呢，忽然來了一個警察，他
　　問我，那隻雞是哪兒偷來的。

24.我很生氣的說：「我是一個誠實的青年。這隻雞是
　　買來的，不是偷來的。」

25.他說，住在我們左邊兒的王先生家，昨天夜裏讓
　　賊偷了很多東西。

26.除了金的跟銀的東西以外，那個賊另外還偷了一
　　隻雞。

27.警察走了以後，老何問我，那隻雞是不是偷來的。

28.我用力的推了他一下說：「你也以為我是賊嗎？」

29.老何拉着我說：「別鬧，別鬧我是跟你開玩笑的。」

30.我大學畢業已經快二十年了，可是每次吃雞的時
　　候還想起來我的老朋友。

Vocabulary

New characters:

隻　雞　蛋　肉　趣
青　相　鬧　重　主
普　通　力　拉　尺
忽　推　惜　誠　懶

---

1. 隻　　　　JR̄/zhī　　　　M: (for animals, birds, etc.)

2. 雞　　　　JĪ　　　　N: chicken

3. 雞蛋　　　JĪDÀN　　　N: (chicken) egg
   蛋　　　　DÀN　　　　N: egg

4. 肉　　　　RÒU　　　　N: meat, flesh

5. 有興趣　YǑU SYÌNGCHYÙ/you xingqu SV/VO: be interested
   趣　　　　CHYÙ/qù　　　　interest　　　　　　　　　in

6. 年青　　NYÁNCHĪNG/niánqīng SV: be young
   青　　　　CHĪNG/qīng　SV: be (dark) green, blue,
   　　　　　　　　　　　　　　　　　　　　black
7. 相當　　SYĀNGDĀNG/xiāngdāng A: fairly
   相　　　　SYĀNG/xiāng　　　　mutual

8. 熱鬧　　RÈNAU/rènao　SV: be bustling, lively, noisy
   鬧　　　　NÀU/nào　　　SV: be noisy

9. 重要　　JÙNGYÀU/zhòngyao SV: be important
   重　　　　JÙNG/zhòng　SV: be heavy

10. dyàu魚　DYÀUYÚ/diàoyú　VO: fish

11. 主意　　JǓYÌ/zhǔyì　　N: idea, plan, suggestion

	主	JŪ/zhǔ	master; host; main
12.	比方說	BǏFĀNGSHWŌ/bǐfāngshuō	MA: for instance
13.	普通	PǓTŪNG/pǔtōng	SV: be common, general
	普	PǓ	general
	通	TŪNG/tōng	all, universal
14.	用力	YÙNGLÌ/yònglì	A: make a strong effort to
	力	LÌ	strength
15.	往上一拉	WÀNG SHÀNG YÌLĀ	PH: to pull up immediately
	拉	LĀ	FV: pull
16.	青	CHĪNG/qīng	SV: be blus
17.	重	JÙNG/zhòng	SV: be heavy
18.	尺	CHŘ/chǐ	M: (Chinese) foot. About 14 inches
19.	忽然	HŪRÁN	MA: suddenly
	忽	HŪ	sudden
20.	推	TWĒI/tūi	FV: push
21.	動	DÙNG/dòng	FV: to move, wiggle
22.	dyàu下去	DYÀUSYACHYÙ/diàoxiàqu	RV: drop, fall
23.	可惜	KĚSYÌ/kěxī	MA/SV: unfortunately/be pitiful, pitiable
	惜	SYĪ/xī	pity
24.	誠實	CHÉNGSHŘ/chéngshí	SV: be honest, sincere
	誠	CHÉNG	honest
25.	早就	DZĂUJYÒU/zǎojiù	A: a long while ago
26.	不好意思	BÙHĂUYÌSZ/bùhǎoyìsi	SV: be embarrassed
27.	lyàng	LYÀNG/liàng	M: (for cars)
28.	主張	JǓJĀNG/zhǔzhāng	FV: suggest, be of opinion that, advocate

29.	交通	*JYAUTŪNG/jiāotōng* N: communications
30.	出主意	*CHŪ JÚYI/chū zhúyi* VO: suggest a plan
31.	懶	*LǍN* SV: lazy
32.	一直	*YÌJŔ/yìzhí* A: all the time, always
33.	青年	*CHĪNGNYÁN/qīngnián* N: young person, youth
34.	推了他一下	*TWĒILE TĀ YÍSYÀ/tūile tā yíxià* PH: give him a push
35.	別鬧	*BYÉNÀU/biénào* PH: don t make a row
36.	開玩笑	*KĀI WÁNSYÀU/kāi wánxiào* VO: make fun of

LESSON 13

Characters	Explanations	Expressions
熟	*SHÚ* SV: be very familiar; ripe; be cooked, done	熟人 N: acquaintance 熟朋友 N: old friend
政	*JÈNG* BF: government, administration zhèng	政客 N: politician 行政 N: administration
府	*FÚ* BF: mansion	府上 IE: polite term for 'your residence' 政府 N: the government, the administration
組 组	*DZŬ* /M: organize/group, section zǔ	小組 N: small group, small unit
織 织	*JŔ* V: weave (cloth, etc.) zhí	組織 V/N: organize/ organization 織布 VO: weave the cloth

Characters	Explanations	Expressions
口	*KǑU* BF: mouth, an opening	人口 N: population 海口 N: seaport 門口ル PW: entrance, a doorway 幾口人 Ph: how many people (in a family)
倍	*-BÈI* M: times, -fold	一倍 NU-M: twice
解	*JYĚ* *jiě* V: loosen, untie	解決 V: solve 了解 V: understand 解放 V: emancipate, liberate
縣 县	*SYÀN* *xiàn* N: a hsien, district (roughly equivalent to a county in the U. S.)	縣長 N: the Magistrate 縣政府 N: district government
市	*SHÌ* *shì* N: municipality	上海市 N: the city of Shanghai 市長 N: mayor 市政府 N: municipal government 市價 N: the market price 黑市 N: the black market price

Characters	Explanations	Expressions
產 产	*CHǍN* BF: products, produce	出產　V/N: produce/ 　　　　products 共產　V: practice 　　　communism 產業　N: real estate, 　　　property
鐵 铁	*TYĚ* N: iron *tiě*	鐵門　N: iron gate 鐵路　N: a railway
葉 叶	*YÈ* BF: leaf	樹葉子　N: leaf 茶葉　N: tea leaves
各	*GÈ* SP: each, every, all	各種各樣　Ph: every kind 各人　N: each person 各處　N: everywhere 各國　N: each nation
計 计	*JÌ* BF: reckon	計算　V: reckon 算計　V: reckon

Characters	Explanations	Expressions
劃 划	HWÀ huà BF: plan	計劃 V/N: plan
或	HWÒ huò BF: either, or	或是 MA: either, or
注	JÙ zhù BF: pay attention	注意 VO/AV/V: pay atten- tion/pay attention to/pay attention 注重 V: emphasize
團 团	TWÁN tuán N: corps, club	旅行團 N: travel club 團體 N: organization
加	JYĀ jiā V: add, increase	參加 V: participate in, join 加起來 RV: add up 小費加一 Ph: including ten per cent tip

第十三課　故　事

　　王先生給小王寫了一封信，要他請張家到西湖[1]去玩兒。小王接着了信就立刻到張家去，把那封信給他們看。張小姐看了信很高興的說。

　　「讓我們計劃[2]，計劃，組織[3]一個旅行團[4]。我想一定有很多同學要來參加[5]。」

　　張先生問小王說：「你在上海的時候一定常到西湖去，那兒的情形你一定很熟[6]。請你給我們講一講，去旅行一次大概需要幾天，費錢不費錢。」

　　小王說：「西湖在Hángjōu市[7]的城外頭。Hángjōu從前是縣[8]，現在 gǎi[9] 成市了。地方不算太大。人口[10]有一百多萬[11]。出產[12]除了茶葉[13]以外，還有……」

　　「夠了，夠了，」張小姐說，「我們對西湖的地理不太有興趣，你能不能講一點兒別的？」

　　小王停了一停說：「從上海到Hángjōu 有一條鐵路[14]，一條公路[15]，所以交通問題很容易解決[16]。或是坐火車去，或是[17]坐汽車去都可以。西湖的風景比北jīng的好十幾倍[18]。各處[19]都有花兒，各處都有草地，湖邊兒上還有各種各樣[20]的石頭。還有那個西湖飯dyàn[21]，

房間又大又乾淨，價錢也不貴，所以每年春天跟秋天，房間總是滿的。」

張小姐說：「按你說，西湖的甚麼都比北jīng的好，恐怕連西湖的月lyang 都比北jīng好。西湖這麼好，你爲甚麼要到北jīng來念書呢？」

「北jīng當然有北jing的好處。」小王gǎn 緊說，「我的意思是西湖的風景跟別的地方不太一樣。」

張太太說：「請你告訴我們，到西湖去玩兒，每人大概需要多少錢？」

小王想了半天說：「這個問題我從來沒注意過，對不起，我不能回答。」

張先生說：「請你給你父母寫一封信，告訴他們，學校一放假我們就去。最好請他們在西湖飯dyàn預先給我們定兩間房間。」

小王說：「沒有問題，沒有問題，我立刻寫信。」

第十三課　句　子

1. 聽說你是一個<u>俄國</u>留學生，你對<u>俄國</u>的情形一定很熟吧。

2. 請你告訴我，<u>俄國</u>政府²⁵的組織跟<u>中國</u>政府的一樣嗎？

3. 聽說<u>中國</u>的人口比<u>俄國</u>的多好幾倍，是真的嗎？

4. <u>俄國</u>也有省，縣跟市嗎？<u>俄國</u>的縣政府跟市政府的組織跟<u>中國</u>的一樣嗎？

5. 我知道<u>俄國</u>出產銅跟鐵，可是我不知道<u>俄國</u>也出產茶葉。

6. 我在<u>北海大學</u>學習歷史跟地理，可是我對各國政府的組織特別有興趣。

7. 我畢業以後計劃暫時在縣政府作一年事。以後或是到<u>德國</u>去留學，或是到<u>美國</u>去留學。

8. 我希望縣政府派我到<u>美國</u>去參觀。我現在對<u>英</u>文很注意，天天在練習。

9. 你知道不知道現在<u>美</u>金的市價²⁶是多少？

10. 站在教堂門口²⁸的，穿深黃皮鞋的那個人，你認識

嗎？他是上海市的市長[29]，我跟他很熟。

11.他組織了一個春假旅行團，打算到各處去旅行。
　　他已經請我參加了。

12.我們計劃先到西湖去玩兒，再到廣東省風景好的
　　地方去看看，最後到北jīng去參觀。

13.交通問題很容易解決，或是坐飛機，或是坐火車
　　都成。

14.從這兒到西湖去，有兩條鐵路，都是省政府辦的。

15.我們旅行團剛才規定，只是結婚的人可以參加，
　　你結婚了沒有？

16.你想見見那位市長嗎？我可以給你們介紹介紹。

17.市政府後頭的那所大樓就是他家。

18.房子前頭有一個大鐵門，門口有草地，牆是淺紅
　　顏色的，很容易找。

19.我們旅行團原來計劃上個月到西湖去。

20.可是因爲我着了點兒涼，得在家裏休息，所以把
　　原來的計劃gǎi了。

21.醫生試了試我的溫度，又給我照了一張X光像。

22.醫生叫我不要chōu烟，不要講話[30]，並且叫護士注
　　意我的溫度。

23.醫生說，我的身體，精神都不好。他要我常到公
　　園去打球。

24.我每天或是吃一隻雞，或是吃半打雞蛋，有的時
　　候也吃肉。

25.現在參加我們旅行團的人 ywè 來 ywè 多了，比上
　　個月多了一倍。

26.各省的人都有，有的我熟，有的我不熟。

27.我知道西湖出產茶葉，除了茶葉以外我不知道還
　　有甚麼別的出產。

28.這次旅行各人得自已解決吃跟住的問題。

29.要是有的人自已不能解決，可以跟我商量，我可
　　以幫他們解決。

30.市長已經叫我注意這件事了。他要我好好兒的計
　　劃計劃。

Vocabulary

New characters:

計　劃　組　織　團
加　熟　市　縣　口
產　葉　鐵　解　或
倍　各　注　政　府

---

1. 西湖　　　　SYĪHÚ/xīhú　　　　　　PW: West Lake

2. 計劃　　　　JÌHWÀ/jìhua　　　　　FV/N: plan
   計　　　　　JÌ　　　　　　　　　　plan, recken
   劃　　　　　HWÀ/huà　　　　　　　plan

3. 組織　　　　DZǓJŔ/zǔzhí　　　　　FV/N: organize/organization
   組　　　　　DZǓ/zǔ　　　　　　　organize
   織　　　　　JŔ/zhí　　　　　　　weave

4. 旅行團　　　LYǙSYÍNGTWÁN/lusyingtuan N: travel club
   團　　　　　TWÁN/tuán　　　　　　club, corps

5. 參加　　　　TSĀNJYĀ/cānjīa　　FV: participate in, join
   加　　　　　JYĀ/jiā　　　　　　FV: add, increase

6. 熟　　　　　SHÚ (sometimes SHÓU) SV: be very familar with

7. Hángjōu 市 HÁNGJŌUSHŔ/Hángzhōushì PW: city of Hangchow
   市　　　　　SHŔ/shì　　　　　　　BF: city

8. 縣　　　　　SYÀN/xiàn　　　　　　N: hsien, district, county

9. gǎi 成　　　GǍICHÉNG　　　　　　RV: change into

10.	人口	RÉNKǑU	N: population
	口	KǑU	mouth; opening
11.	一百多萬	YĪBǍIDWŌWÀN/yìbǎiduōwàn	NU-M more than one million
12.	出產	CHŪCHǍN	FV/N: produce/products
	產	CHǍN	FV: produce
13.	茶葉	CHÁYÈ	N: tea leaves
	葉	YÈ	leaf
14.	鐵路	TYĚLÙ/tiělù	N: railroad
	鐵	TYĚ/tiě	N: iron
15.	公路	GŪNGLÙ/gōnglù	N: highway
16.	解決	JYĚJYWÉ/jiějué	FV: solve
	解	JYĚ/jiě	loosen, untie
17.	或是…或是	HWÒSHR ... HWÒSHR huòshi ... huòshi	PAT: either ... or ...
	或	HWÒ/huò	either, or
18.	倍	-BÈI	M: -time, -fold
19.	各處	GÈCHÙ	PW: everywhere
	各	GÈ-	SP: each-, every-
20.	各種各樣	GÈJǓNG GÈYÀNG/gèzhǒng gèyàng	PH: every kind
21.	西湖飯dyàn	SYĪHÚ FÀNDYÀN/xīhú fàndiàn	N: West Lake Hotel
22.	月lyang	YWÈLYANG/yuèliang	N: moon
23.	gǎn 緊	GǍNJǏN	A: hurriedly, at once
24.	注意	JÙYÌ/zhùyì	VO/AV/FV: pay attention to
	注	JÙ/zhù	pay attention
25.	政府	JÈNGFǓ/zhèngfǔ	N: government
	政	JÈNG/zhèng	administration
	府	FǓ	mansion

26.	市價	SHRJYÀ/shìjià	N: market price
27.	黑市	HĒISHÌ/hēishì	N: black market
28.	門口	MÉNKŎU	N: gateway, doorway
29.	市長	SHRJĂNG/shìzhǎng	N: mayor
30.	講話	JYĂNGHWÀ/jiǎnghuà	VO: talk
31.	各人	GÈREN	N: every person, each person

LESSON 14

Characters	Explanations	Expressions
無 无	*WÚ* BF: without, have not	無數 M: innumerable 無政府 N: anarchy

論
论
	LWÙN BF: discuss, argue,
	lùn speak of
		無論 A: no matter what,
		           it does not
		           matter
		論文 N: essay
		社論 N: editorial

俗	*SÚ* SV: be vulgar, common	風俗 N: custom 俗話 N: common saying
慣 惯	*GWÀN* SV: be accustomed guàn	習慣 N: habits

全	*CHWÁN A/SV* all, entirely/
	quán be complete
		完全 A/SV: perfectly,
		             completely/
		             be perfect,
		             complete
		全世界 N: the whole world

162

Characters	Explanations	Expressions
化	*HWÀ* BF: [V: melt] *hùa*	文化　　　N: culture, civilization 科學化　SV: scientific 化學　　　N: chemistry
濟 济	*JÌ* BF: [aid]	經濟　　　　N/SV: economy/be economical 經濟學　　　N: economics 經濟學家 N: economist
向	*SYÀNG* CV/BF: face towards/ hitherto *xiàng*	向來　　　MA: hitherto, habitually
較 较	*JYǍU* BF: compare *jiǎo*	比較　　　V/A: compare/ comparatively
線 线 綫	*SYÀN* N: line; thread *xiàn*	無線電 收音機　N: radio receiving set 直線　　　N: straight line 電線　　　N: wire 航線　　　N: aviation route; navigation route

Characters	Explanations	Expressions
器	**CHÌ** BF: tool, implement, vessel qì	機器 N: machine, engine 鐵器 N: hardware, iron tools 銀器 N: silverware
類 类	**LÈI** M: kind, class, category	分三類 Ph: divided into three categories 種類 N: kind, species
輕 轻	**CHĪNG** be light (in weight) qīng	輕重 N: weight
油	**YǑU** N: oil; sauce	石油 N: petroleum 原油 N: crude oil 汽油 N: gasoline
將 将	**JYĀNG** to be about to jiāng	將來 MA: in the future

Characters	Explanations	Expressions
言	*YÁN* BF: language	文言 N: literary language (classical style) 語言 N: language
香	*SYĀNG* SV: be fragrant, smell good xiāng	香水 N: perfume
切	*CHYÈ* BF: all, entirely qiè	一切 N: the whole lot
裝 裝	*JWĀNG* V: pack, load zhuāng	裝備 N: equipment (military)
迎	*YÍNG* BF: welcome, go to meet	歡迎 V/N: welcome 歡迎會 N: welcome meeting

第十四課　故　事

　　有一個夏天的下午，太陽很好，小王約張小姐
到鄉下去玩兒。他們帶了很多吃的東西，張小姐還
帶了一個小無線電收音機。小王把一切東西都裝在
汽車裏，兩個人開着車就到鄉下去了。他們到了鄉
下以後，在湖邊兒的草地上找了一個合適的地方，
就坐下來，一邊兒吃東西，一邊兒談話。他們談了
一會兒中國的文化，張小姐覺得沒有甚麼興趣。張
小姐說：

　　「我對中國的文化向來沒注意過，我們不如談一
點兒有興趣的事情。」

　　小王說：「好，我們談談科學吧。」

　　張小姐說：「我不是一個科學家，我對科學也沒
有興趣。」

　　小王跟張小姐談了一會兒中國各處的風俗，習
慣跟語言，張小姐還覺得沒有興趣。

　　張小姐問小王說：「你將來畢業以後打算作甚麼
呢？」

　　小王說：「我想到德國去學經濟。你呢？」

張小姐說:「我還沒有決定，也許到一個航空公司去作事; 也許……」

「要是你願意,」小王說,「我們……」

那個時候他們忽然聽見樹後頭有人說話:「já雞的味兒眞香!」

他們一聽就知道是小李的聲音。

「你到這兒來作甚麼?」小王問。

「我原來計劃到縣政府去看一個朋友，可是我的汽車在路上停了。我以爲機器壞了，收拾了半天才知道是汽油沒有了。我想把車推回去，可是這lyàng舊車眞不輕。我用力推了半天，推不動。所以我到這兒來看看，也許我的運氣好，看見熟人。沒想到看見你們了，不知道你們歡迎不歡迎我參加。」

小王還沒回答，張小姐說:「歡迎，歡迎，你請坐吧。」

張小姐說完了就從hé子裏取出一包já雞，交給小李。張小姐跟小李一會兒談電影，一會兒談聽戲，一會兒又談運動。小王對這類東西都沒有興趣，所以不很高興。

小王說:「這兒的風景很普通，我們到別的地方

去吧。小李，要是你計劃到縣政府去看朋友，我可以借給你一點兒汽油。」

小李說:「縣政府今天去不去沒有關係。並且現在已經四點鐘了，到縣政府去恐怕太晚了。我跟你們一塊兒去玩兒吧。」

晚上小王跟小李送張小姐回家。小李說:「今天玩兒得真有意思。以後你們再出去玩兒，別忘了告訴我。」

小王看了一看小李，沒說甚麼，就走了。

個時候汽油的價錢很低。

也父親常常給他講中國的故事。他父親說，中國
是全世界最有意思的地方。

也小的時候就希望他將來能到中國去。

也昨天到我家來，問了我很多關yu中國的情形。[29]

也先問我中國人的風俗，習慣，後來又問我中國
的歷史跟文化。

我說，中國人的風俗，習慣，跟德國人的，完全
不一樣。

我又說，我對中國的文化向來很有興趣，可是不
敢說有研究。

我們又談了關yu中國的語言，特別是文言。[30]

我說，中國各省的語言都不同。中國的文言很難
懂。[31][32]

他問我：「文言跟俗話一樣嗎？」我說，文言跟俗
話完全不同。[33]

他又問我現在中國的經濟情形。我說，我對經濟
沒有甚麼研究。

我問他，喜歡不喜歡吃中國飯。他說，他向來喜
歡吃中國飯。

第十四課　句　子

1.無論是誰，要是他要到中國去，他得先
　兒中國人的風俗習慣。

2.我有一個德國朋友，他要到中國去組織
　公司。

3.可是他對中國人的風俗習慣完全不清楚

4.他對中國文化，跟中國社會的經濟情形
　知道。

5.可是他向來喜歡跟中國人在一塊兒作事

6.他說，中國的地方那麼大，人口這麼多
　國都不能跟中國比較。

7.他說，他父親從前在中國作買賣，他賣
　也賣機器。

8.無線電收音機的種類很多；有的是美國
　的是德國式的。

9.美國式的收音機比較重；德國式的收音

10.機器的種類也很多：有的是飛機的機器
　汽車的機器。

11.他父親除了賣機器以外也賣汽油。他父

23.中國飯的味兒香極了。將來有機會，他想學學怎麼作。

24.我問他，行李收拾好了沒有。他說，一切都收拾好了。

26.他這次坐飛機走，所以行李很輕。

26.他把一切東西都裝在一個syāng 子裏。他說，那個syāng子已經滿了。

27.他說，他在中國有很多朋友。他們一定會到飛機場去歡迎他。

28.我請他給我帶一點兒東西到中國去。他問我，是哪一類的東西？輕不輕？

29.我說，是一點兒俄國出產的茶葉，我已經裝在一個小hé子裏了。

30.他說：「成，無論甚麼都成，你交給我吧。」

Vocabulary

New characters:

無　　線　　切　　裝　　化

向　　俗　　慣　　言　　將

濟　　香　　器　　油　　輕

迎　　類　　論　　全　　較

1.	無線電收 音機	*WÚSYÀNDYÀN SHŌUYĪNJĪ*　N: *radio set* *wúxiàndiàn shōuyīnjī*	
	無	*WÚ*	*without, have not*
	線	*SYÀN/xiàn*	N: *line; wire; thread*
2.	一切	*YÍCHYÈ/yíqiè*	N: *the whole lot*
	切	*CHYÈ/qiè*	*all, entire*
3.	裝	*JWĀNG/zhuāng*	FV: *pack; load*
4.	文化	*WÉNHWÀ/wénhuà*	N: *culture, civilization*
	化	*HWÀ/huà*	FV: *melt*
5.	向來	*SYÀNGLÁI/xiànglái* MA: *hitherto, always*
	向	*SYÀNG/xiàng*	*hitherto, up to now*
6.	風俗	*FĒNGSÚ*	N: *custom (of a people)*
	俗	*SÚ*	SV: *common, vulgar*
7.	習慣	*SYÍGWÀN/xíguàn*	N: *habit (of a person or people)*
	慣	*GWÀN/guàn*	SV: *be accostomed to*
8.	語言	*YŬYÁN*	N: *language*
	言	*YÁN*	*language*

9.	將來	JYĀNGLÁI/jiānglái	MA: in the future
	將	JYĀNG/jiāng	about to
10.	經濟	JĪNGJI	N: economics
	濟	JÌ	aid
11.	já雞	JÁJĪ/zhájī	N: fried chicken
12.	香	SYĀNG/xiāng	SV: smell good
13.	機器	JĪCHÌ/jīqì	N: machine, engine
	器	CHÌ/qì	tool
14.	收拾	SHŌUSHR/shōushi	FV: repair, fix up
15.	汽油	CHÌYÓU/qìyóu	N: gasoline
	油	YÓU	N: oil; sauce; grease
16.	輕	CHĪNG/qīng	SV: be light in weight
17.	推不動	TWĒIBUDÙNG/tuībudòng	RV: unable to move by pushing
18.	運氣	YÙNCHI/yùnqi	N: luck
19.	歡迎	HWĀNYÍNG/huānyíng	FV: welcome, greet
	迎	YÍNG	go to meet
20.	hé子	HÉDZ/hézi	N: (small) box
21.	類	LÈI	M: category
22.	無論	WÚLWÙN/wúlùn	A: no matter what ... it does not matter ...
	論	LWÙN/lùn	discuss, speak of
23.	完全	WÁNCHYWÁN/wánquán	A/SV: all, entirely/ be complete
	全	CHYWÁN/quán	A/SV: entirely/be complete
24.	比較	BǏJYÀU/bǐjiǎo	FV/A: compare/comparatively
	較	JYÀU/jiǎo	compare
25.	無線電	WÚSYÀNDYÀN/wúxiàndiàn	N: radio
26.	種類	JǓNGLÈI/zhǒnglèi	N: kind, species

27.	美國式	MĚIGWÒSHR̀/Měiguóshì	AT: American style
28.	收音機	SHŌUYĪNJĪ	N: radio
29.	關yu	GWĀNYU/guānyu	CV: about, concerning
30.	文言	WÉNYÁN	N: literary language (classical style)
31.	各省	GÈSHĚNG	N; every province
32.	不同	BÙTÚNG/bùtóng	SV: be different
33.	俗話	SÚHWÀ/súhùa	N: common saying, proverb
34.	syāng子	SYĀNGDZ/xiāngzi	N: suitcase; trunk

LESSON 15

Characters	Explanations	Expressions
軍 军	*JWŪN* BF: military jun	海軍　　N: Navy 空軍　　N: Air Force 將軍　　N: general 軍事　　N: military
基	*JĪ*　BF: base	基地　　N: base 空軍基地 N: air base 基本　　SV: basic
陸 陆	*LÙ*　BF: land	陸地　　N: land (as dis- 　　　　　tinguished from 　　　　　the sea) 大陸　　N: continent 陸軍　　N: Army
部	*BÙ*　M: part, section	北部　　N: north part 一部分　M: a part 陸軍部　N: Department of 　　　　　Army 外交部　N: Ministry of 　　　　　Foreign Affairs
洋	*YÁNG* N/BF: ocean/foreign	太平洋　PW: the Pacific 　　　　　Ocean 大西洋　PW: the Atlantic 　　　　　Ocean 洋火　　N: matches

Characters	Explanations	Expressions
架	*JYÀ* BF/M: framework/(measure for airplane) *jià*	一架飛機 N: an airplane 書架　　 N: book shelf 架子　　 N: frame
員 员	*YWÁN* BF: personnel *yuán*	飛行員 N: flier, aviator 人員　 N: personnel 動員　 V: mobilize
降	*JYĀNG* descend *jiāng*	降下來 V: descend
落	*LWÒ* V: alight, land, come down *luò*	降落　　 V: land (form the air) 落下來 V: drop down; fall (as leaves)
據 据	*JYÙ* CV: according to *jù*	據說　　 IE: it is said, it's reported 據他說 Ph: according to what he said

Characters	Explanations	Expressions
危	*WĒI*　BF: dangerous	危險　N/SV: danger/be dangerous, critical 危機　N: crisis of danger; critical point
民	*MÍN*　BF: people	人民　N: people 國民　N: national, people 公民　N: citizen 民主　SV: be democratic 民主國家　N: democratic nation
蘇 苏	*SŪ*　BF: Soviet Union	蘇俄　N: Soviet Russia
聯 联	*LYÁN* BF: unite *lián*	蘇聯　N: Soviet Union 聯軍　N: allied force 聯合國　N: The United Nations
雜 杂	*DZǍ*　SV: be mixed, *zá*　　 miscellaneous	雜誌　N: magazine

Characters	Explanations	Expressions
誌 志	JR **BF:** record zhì	雜誌 **N:** magazine
救	JYOU **V:** save, rescue jiù	救人 **VO:** rescue people 救火 **VO:** extinguish a fire
助	JU **BF:** aid, help zhù	幫助 **N/V:** help
目	MU **BF:** [L: eye] 	目的 mùdì **N:** purpose, aim, goal 題目 **N:** topic, theme
消	SYAU **BF:** diminish, consume xiāo	消息 **N:** news, information

第十五課　故事

　　有一天小王到張家去找張小姐。張小姐沒在家，可是小李在那兒。小李說，張小姐到銀行去取錢去了。小王說:

「我明天要考試，我得立刻回學校去。」

　　小李說:「我們旣然來了，坐一會兒吧，反正外頭下着雨呢。」

　　小王跟小李坐下以後，兩個人很久沒說話。後來小王說:

「這兩天報上有一個很重要的消息¹，你看見了沒有？」

「你說的是那架²蘇聯³飛機dyàu 在太平洋⁴西部⁵的消息嗎？」小李問。

「對了，據說是機器壞了⁶。我們的海軍⁷已經派了一隻船幫助⁸他們去救人⁹去了。」

「據今天的報上說，他們發現那個飛行員¹⁰已經死了。我覺得那是很普通的消息，你爲甚麼說這個消息很重要呢？」小李問。

「我剛聽到那個消息的時候也覺得是一個很普通

的消息，可是後來我ywè 想ywè 覺得那個消息不簡
單。你想想，那架蘇聯飛機是從哪兒起飛的？到太
平洋上去的目的是甚麼？」

「你的意思是……」

「可不是嗎？」小王很高興的說，「據我看，蘇聯
在離中國北部不遠的地方一定有一個空軍基地。那
架飛機一定是從那個基地起飛的。起飛的目的一定
是想試一試飛機上的汽油夠不夠飛到中國再飛回去。」

「有理，有理。」小李覺得小王的意思對極了，「前
幾天有一本雜誌上說，"蘇聯的陸軍比我們的多好幾
倍，目的是要解放全世界。"要"解放"全世界一定先
得"解放"中國。我看中國將來相當危險。」

小王說：「最危險的是中國政府對這樣重要的消
息一點兒也沒注意，並且派海軍去幫助他們救人，
你說奇怪不奇怪。」

「小王，我們都是中國的國民，我想我們應當把
我們的意思告訴政府。」

「小李，你說得對，我們明天到市政府去見見市
長，怎麼樣？」

張小姐回來的時候，看見他們兩個人ywè 說ywè

高興。好像全世界就他們兩個人知道怎麼救<u>中國</u>。

第十五課　句子

1. 一年以前我在一個空軍基地作事。

2. 那個基地在中國大陸的北部，離太平洋就有一百公里。

3. 那個基地一共有五百架飛機，每一架飛機有一個或是兩個飛行員。

4. 每一分鐘有很多飛機起飛，每一分鐘也有很多飛機降落。

5. 因爲我的身體不太好，所以我不是一個飛行員。

6. 據說，飛行員很苦，每天得練習起飛跟降落。

7. 據說，要是降落的時候不小心，很危險。

8. 在基地作事的人都是中國公民。不是中國公民就不能在基地作事。

9. 據說，離我們的基地不遠，有一個蘇聯的陸軍基地。

10. 我不知道那個陸軍基地有多少人。據說，比我們這兒的人多好幾倍。

11. 我看見一本雜誌上說，蘇聯現在可以動員三百萬陸軍。

12.可是全世界的民主國家只能動員一百五十萬陸軍。

13.據那本雜誌說，我們政府已經請聯合國注意這件事了。

14.我們那兒各種雜誌都有，可是我最喜歡看空軍雜誌。

15.我是一個喜歡安靜的人。我最怕熱鬧。我常常一個人坐在綠樹底下，聽鳥兒叫。

16.有一天我正坐在樹底下看雜誌呢，忽然聽見有人叫我。

17.那個人說，剛才有一架蘇聯的飛機要在我們的基地降落。

18.可是那架飛機飛到我們的基地以前，汽油已經用完了，所以dyàu在太平洋上了。

19.我們已經派了兩架飛機去救了。據說現在太平洋上的天氣非常不好。

20.我不懂，爲甚麼我們的飛機要幫助蘇聯，救他們的飛機。

21.後來我們的飛機回來了。我等他們降落以後，就跑過去問他們。

22.他們說，他們看見那架飛機了，可是沒看見飛行

員。

23.他們的目的是去救那個飛行員，不是去救那架飛
機。

24.後來我聽到無線電收音機裏的消息說，那個蘇聯
的飛行員已經讓美國海軍給救了。

25.美國在日本的西部有好幾個海軍基地。

26.據說，那個飛行員現在在日本西南部的一個醫院
裏。

27.他不願意回蘇聯去。他說，回蘇聯去太危險，他
們一定會清算他。

28.他請美國政府幫助他，把他送到美國的西部去。

29.他說，他要到美國去的目的，將來他可以作一個
美國公民。

30.他說，蘇聯空軍的一切他都知道得很清楚，他可
以給美國政府很多幫助。

Vocabulary

New characters:

消　架　蘇　聯　洋
部　據　**軍**　助　救
員　目　基　雜　誌
陸　危　民　降　落

---

1. 消息　　　SYĀUSYI/xiāoxi　　　N: news, information
　　消　　　SYĀU/xiāo　　　　　　diminish
2. 架　　　　JYÀ/jià　　　　　　　M: (for airplanes)
3. 蘇聯　　　SŪLYÁN/Sūlián　　　PW: Soviet Union
　　蘇　　　SŪ　　　　　　　　　　Soviet Union
　　聯　　　LYÁN/lián　　　　　　unite
4. 太平洋　　TÀIPÍNGYÁNG　　　　PW: Pacific Ocean
　　洋　　　YÁNG　　　　　　　　　　ocean
5. 部　　　　BÙ　　　　　　　　　　M: part, section
6. 據說　　　JYÙSHWŌ/jùshūo　　　IE: it is said that
　　據　　　JYÙ/jù　　　　　　　　CV: according to
7. 海軍　　　HĂIJYŪN/hǎijūn　　　N: navy
　　軍　　　JYŪN/jūn　　　　　　　　military
8. 幫助　　　BĀNGJÙ/bāngzhù　　　FV: help, assist
　　助　　　JÙ/zhù　　　　　　　　　help, assist
9. 救　　　　JYÒU/jìu　　　　　　　FV: save, rescue
10. 飛行員　FĒISYÍNGYWÁN/fēixíngyúan N: flier, aviator

員	YWÁN/yuán	personel
11. 我ywè想ywè 學得...	WǑ YWÈ SYǍNG YWÈ JYWÉDE wǒ yuè xiǎng yuè juéde	PAT: the more I think, the more I feel
12. 目的	MÙDI	N: purpose, aim, goal
目	MÙ	eye
13. 可不是嗎	KÉBÚSHR MA/kébùshì ma	IE: sure enough
14. 空軍基地	KŪNGJYŪNDÌ/kōngjūndì	A: air base
空軍	KŪNGJYŪN/kōngjūn	N: air force
基地	JĪDÌ	N: base
基	JĪ	base
15. 有理	YǑULǏ	SV: be logical, reasonable
16. 雜誌	DZÁJR/zázhì	N: magazine
雜	DZÁ/zá	miscellaneous
誌	JR/zhì	record
17. 陸軍	LÙJYŪN/lùjūn	A: army
陸	LÙ	land
18. 多好幾倍	DWŌ HǍUJǏBÈI/duō hǎojǐbèi	PH: be several times more
19. 解放	JYĚFÀNG/jiěfàng	FV: liberate, make free
20. 危險	WĒISYǍN/wēixiǎn	SV/N: be dangerous/ danger
危	WĒI	dangerous
21. 國民	GWÓMÍN/guómín	N: national, people
民	MÍN	people
22. 大陸	DÀLÙ	N: continent
23. 降落	JYÀNGLWÒ/jiàngluò	FV: land (from the air)
降	JYÀNG/jiàng	descend
落	LWÒ/luò	FV: come down
24. 公民	GŪNGMÍN/gōngmín	N: citizen, citizenry

25. 動員　　　　DÙNGYWÁN/dòngyuán　　　FV: mobilize

26. 民主國家　　MÍNJŬGWÓJYĀ/mínzhǔguójiā N: democratic nation

　　　民主　　　MÍNJŬ/mínzhǔ　　　　SV/N: be democratic/democ-
                                                                racy
27. 聯合國　　　LYÁNHÉGWÓ/liánhéguó N: The United Nations

28. 清算　　　　CHĪNGSWÀN/qīngsuàn FV: liquidate, purge

300 Characters Introduced in Read Chinese I

1-3 STROKES	ROMANIZATION	LESSON									
			也	yě	1	太	tài	9	为	wèi <wéi>	6
一	yī	1	山	shān	17	友	yǒu	6	认	rèn	14
又	yòu	8	千	chyān	10	不	bù	1	什	shém <shèn>	2
二	èr	1	女	nyǔ	10	少	shǎu	3	办	bàn	16
十	shŕ	1	儿	ér	2	以	yǐ	5	书	shū	7
七	chī	1	几	jǐ	6	日	r̀	5	**5**		
了	le <lyǎu>	2	个	gè	1	比	bǐ	17	半	bàn	6
人	rén	1	万	wàn	10	水	shwěi	13	必	bì	11
八	bā	1	门	mén	8	中	jūng	1	平	píng	15
九	jyǒu	1	么	ma	2	今	jīn	7	打	dǎ	14
三	sān	1	**4**			分	fēn	13	可	kě	4
已	yǐ	13	火	hwǒ	13	父	fù	7	正	jèng	11
己	jǐ	14	六	lyòu	1	月	ywè	1	去	chyù	3
下	syà	1	文	wén	16	手	shǒu	10	本	běn	5
工	gūng	14	方	fāng	2	毛	máu	19	左	dzwǒ	18
子	dž	3	心	syīn	19	开	kāi	13	右	yòu	18
才	tsái	19	王	wáng	19	车	chē	13	北	běi	18
大	dà	1	天	tyān	1	见	jyàn	11	叫	jyàu	6
小	syǎu	1	夫	fū	14	气	chì	11	四	sż	1
上	shàng	1	五	wǔ	1	从	tsúng	8	出	chū	8

外	wài	2	有	yǒu	1	当	dāng	15	走	dzǒu	6
母	mǔ	7	百	bǎi	6	岁	swèi	12	见	jyàn	11
生	shēng	3	在	dzài	2	后	hòu	2	吧	ba	11
用	yùng	4	西	syī	4	会	hwèi	5	别	byé	9
句	jyù	11	老	lǎu	6	欢	hwān	15	男	nán	10
白	bái	13	再	dzài	8	关	gwān	13	坐	dzwò	5
他	tā	1	地	dì	2	问	wèn	5	告	gàn	12
长	cháng	17	早	dzǎu	6	买	mǎi	4	我	wǒ	1
东	dūng	4	因	yīn	9	许	syǔ	19	每	měi	19
旧	jyòu	18	吃	chī	5	7			位	wèi	9
们	mén	1	回	hwéi	5	没	méi	1	住	jù	7
头	tóu	2	名	míng	16	完	wán	16	你	nǐ	1
边	byān	18	多	dwō	3	弟	dì	12	但	dàn	19
对	dwèi	4	年	nyán	8	快	kwài	8	作	dzwò	4
写	syě	5	先	syān	3	忘	wàng	12	近	jìn	18
6			自	dz̀	14	那	nà	2	远	ywǎn	18
字	dz̀	5	件	jyàn	9	車	chē	13	进	jìn	9
忙	máng	18	好	hǎu	3	更	gèng	17	还	hái <hwán>	6
次	tsz̀	17	行	syíng	9	把	bǎ	8	这	jè	2
衣	yī	16	过	gwò	13	找	jǎu	13	吗	ma	2

Char	Pinyin	No.	Char	Pinyin	No.	Char	Pinyin	No.	Char	Pinyin	No.
听	tīng	6	房	fáng	10	念	nyàn	7	送	sùng	9
坏	hwài	16	放	fàng	14	朋	péng	6	差	chà	13
块	kwài	7	夜	yè	12	知	jr̄	8	美	měi	16
报	bàu	13	底	dǐ	14	兒	ér	2	前	chyán	4
饭	fàn	5	刻	kè	13	的	de <dì>	1	穿	chwān	18
时	shŕ	4	長	cháng	17	所	swǒ	7	客	kè	16
来	lái	3	玩	wán	15	姓	syìng	7	為	wèi <wéi>	6
里	lǐ	2	表	byǎu	10	往	wàng	19	屋	wū	10
两	lyǎng	1	事	shř	4	极	jí	17	孩	hái	12
应	yīng	15	東	dūng	4	张	jāng	11	城	chéng	12
纸	jř	10	兩	lyǎng	1	话	hwà	3	要	yàu	3
条	tyáu	17	直	jŕ	18	现	syàn	6	南	nán	18
诉	sùng <sù>	12	來	lái	3	经	jīng	13	甚	shém <shèn>	2
识	shŕ	14	奇	chí	19	国	gwó	3	是	shř	1
8			到	dàu	2	学	sywé	5	昨	dzwó	7
河	hé	17	呢	ne	11	卖	mài	4	思	sz̄	9
法	fà <fá>	16	門	mén	8	画	hwà	17	怎	dzěn	11
定	dìng	11	明	míng	7	鱼	yú	17	星	syīng	9
怪	gwài	19	易	yi	16	9			看	kàn	3
怕	pà	16	些	syē	4				信	syìn	10

便	byàn <pyán>	19	病	bìng	15	紧	jǐn	11	唱	chàng	11
很	hěn	3	書	shū	7	请	chǐng	5	國	gwó	3
後	hòu	2	哥	gē	15	谁	shéi	10	第	dì	7
给	gěi	3	起	chǐ	8	样	yàng	17	夠	gòu	15
说	shwō	3	真	jēn	10	帮	bāng	15	鱼	yú	17
钟	jūng	8	校	syàu	14	钱	chyán	4	進	jìn	9
点	dyǎn	6	時	shŕ	4	难	nán	13	船	chwán	17
觉	jywé <jyàu>	16	哭	kū	15	离	lí	18	得	děi <dé>	13
贵	gwèi	9	茶	chá	14	**11**			從	tsúng	8
亲	chīn	7	笑	syàu	14	着	je <jáu>	8	脸	lyǎn	19
带	dài	15	拿	ná	9	情	chíng	9	馆	gwǎn	18
10			能	néng	5	許	syǔ	19	**12**		
酒	jyǒu	18	氣	chi	11	張	jāng	11	道	dàu	8
家	jyā	7	們	mén	1	現	syàn	6	訴	sùng <sù>	12
容	rúng	16	個	gè	1	教	jyāu <jyàu>	13	就	jyòu	5
站	jàn	12	候	hòu	4	都	dōu <dū>	4	畫	hwà	17
這	jè	2	條	tyáu	17	帶	dài	15	報	bàu	13
高	gāu	11	紙	jř	10	常	cháng	10	喜	syǐ	15
桌	jwō	14	爱	ài	9	問	wèn	5	極	jí	17
哪	ㄋǎ	2	笔	bǐ	10	晚	wǎn	7	期	chī	9

黑	hēi	17	嗎	ma	2	慢	màn	8	辦	bàn	16
最	dzwèi	17	新	syīn	10	說	shwō	3	頭	tóu	2
開	kāi	13	意	yì	6	認	rèn	14	還	hái <hwán>	6
喝	hē	18	話	hwà	3	麼	ma	2	館	gwǎn	18
貴	gwèi	9	裏	lǐ	2	歌	gē	11	錯	tswò	16
跑	pǎu	13	遠	ywǎn	18	緊	jǐn	11	錢	chyán	4
過	gwò	13	塊	kwài	7	對	dwèi	4	學	sywéi	5
菜	tsài	14	想	syǎng	4	算	swàn	14	17		
買	mǎi	4	當	dāng	15	願	ywàn	15	謝	syè	5
飯	fàn	5	睡	shwèi	15	15			應	yǐng	15
筆	bǐ	10	跟	gēn	11	寫	syě	5	幫	bāng	15
等	děng	8	路	lù	15	請	chǐng	5	點	dyǎn	6
然	rán	19	萬	wàn	10	誰	shéi	10	臉	lyǎn	19
短	dwǎn	17	歲	swèi	12	賣	mài	4	18~		
給	gěi	3	愛	ài	9	樣	yàng	17	識	shŕ	14
幾	jǐ	6	會	hwèi	5	數	shù	19	離	lí	18
街	jyē	12	經	jīng	13	鋪	pù	16	壞	hwài	16
铺	pù	16	错	tswò	16	16			聽	tīng	6
谢	syè	5	数	shù	19	懂	dǔng	12	願	ywàn	15
13			14			親	chīn	7	關	gwān	13

歡	hwān	15		鐘	jūng	8
舊	jyòu	18		覺	jywé <jyàu>	16
難	nán	13		邊	byān	18

SERIAL ORDER OF CHARACTERS

Most students find it something of a chore to look up characters in a dictionary. The traditional serial arrangement of Chinese characters according to "radicals" — often arbitrarily assigned — is at best clumsy. It is annoying to have to go through three steps: (i) identification of the radical, (ii) counting the number of remaining strokes and finding the character in a list under the proper radical, and (iii) searching the page indicated for the object of one's search.

A new serial arrangement has grown in favor in recent years and has been adopted by committee of scholars at work on language reform under the Peking regime. While still far from simple, compared with alphabetization, it has certain advantages over the radical-phonetic system.

To look up a character in a dictionary arranged on this plan we first count the total number of strokes in the character — not just the number in the radical. All characters are arranged in groups in the numerical order of their stroke-count. This step is comparable to the use of the 26 letters of our alphabet for grouping words.

Within each of these groups order is determined first by the initial stroke in writing the character. Four such initial strokes are specified:

1. A dot (dyǎr) or longer stroke downward to the right.

方説弟送

2. A horizontal (héngr), including angles which begin with a left-to-right horizontal.

百走書也

VOCABULARY LIST

The following list of characters and combinations is arranged by a combination of stroke-counting and stroke order. In this system a character or a combination is first sorted into a group according to the number of strokes in the character or the number of strokes in the first character in the combination. The group is subdivided according to the value of the first stroke arranged in the order of 1. a dot (﹅) 2. a horizontal stroke (—) 3. a vertical stroke (|) 4. a left downward slant (ノ). Within each subdivision the arrangement is made according to the value of the second stroke, and so on.

1 (一)
				LESSON
一直	yìjŕ	A:	all the time, always	12
一直沒...過	yìjŕ méi...gwò	PAT:	never...	10
一共	yígùng	MA:	altogether	1
一打	yìdá	M:	one dozen	4
一百多萬	yìbǎidwōwàn	NU-M:	more than one million	13
一切	yíchyè	N:	the whole lot	14
一路平安	yílùpíngān	PH:	pleasant journey	2
一邊兒... 一邊兒...	yìbyār...yìbyār	PAT:	on one hand...on the other hand.....	10

2 (一)
二樓	èrlóu	N:	second floor	4
十點零五分	shŕdyǎn-língwǔfēn		five minutes past ten	3
力	lì	BF:	strength, power	12

2 (ノ)
X光	àikeszgwāng	N:	X-ray	10
人口	rénkǒu	N:	population	13

195

3 （一）

下雨	syàyǔ	VO:	rain (falls)	10
下雪	syàsywě	VO:	snow (falls)	8
士	shr̀	BF:	nurse	10
大衣	dàyī	N:	overcoat	4
大家	dàjyā	N:	all; everybody	1
大陸	dàlù	N:	continent	15
大概	dàgài	A:	probably	1
大學	dàsywé	N:	university, college	1
大小	dàsyǎu	N:	size	4
大禮堂	dàlǐtáng	N:	auditorium	8
大聲說話	dàshēng shwōhwá	PH:	speak loudly	5

3 （丨）

上午	shàngwǔ	TW:	forenoon	3
上海	Shànghǎi	TW:	Shanghai	1
上課	shàngkè	VO:	go to classes	8
上di	shàngdì	N:	God	7
口	kǒu	N:	mouth, an opening	13
小姐	syáujye	N:	Miss; polite for daughter	2
小學	shǎusywé	N:	elementary school	1
小聲	syǎushēng	A:	quietly, in a low voice	6

3 （丿）

久	jyǒu	SV:	long (of time)	5

4 （丶）

文言	wényán	N:	literary language	14
文化	wénhwà	N:	culture, civilization	14

4 (一)

尺	*chǐ*	M:	(a chinese foot)	12
天 jing	*Tyānjing*	PW:	Tientsin	3
切	*chyè*	BF:	all, entirely	14
太陽	*tàiyang*	N:	the sun	11
太平洋	*Tàipíngyáng*	PW:	the Pacific Ocean	15
不理	*bùlǐ*	FV:	pay no attention; do not talk to	7
不到	*búdàu*	FV:	less than, not quite	6
不同	*bùdúng*	SV:	be different	14
不如	*bùrú*	FV:	be not as good as	11
不管	*bùgwǎn*	FV:	no matter whether	5
不算	*búswàn*	FV:	cannot be considered	8
不好意思	*bùhǎuyìsz*	SV:	be embarassed	12
不過	*búgwò*	A:	but	7
不久	*bùjyǒu*	A:	before long, not long after	7

4 (丨)

中學	*jūngsywé*	N:	high school	1
以爲	*yǐwéi*	FV:	suppose; take it that	3
比較	*bǐjyǎu*	FV/A:	compare/comparatively	14
比方說	*bǐfāngshwō*	FV:	for instance	12
水管子	*shwěigwǎndz*	N:	water pipe	5

4 (丿)

介	*jyè*	BF:	lie between	1
介紹	*jyèshau*	V:	introduce, recommend	1
公	*gūng*	BF:	public, official	6
公司	*gūngsz̄*	N:	company, corporation	6
公民	*gūngmín*	N:	citizen	15

公里	gūnglǐ	M: a kilometer	6
公路	gūnglù	N: a highway	13
公園	gūngywán	N: park	11
月 lyang	ywèlyang	N: moon	13
午	wǔ	BF: noon	3
化	hwà	FV: melt	14
反	fǎn	BF: the wrong side	7
反正	fǎnjèng	MA: in any case, anyway	7
反對	fǎmdwèi	FV: oppose	7

5 （、）

立	lì	F V: establish; stand	3
立刻	lìkè	A: at once	3
主	jǔ	BF: master, host; main, chief	12
主意	júyi	N: idea, plan	12
主張	jǔjāng	FV: advocate	12
市	shr̀	N: municipality	13
市長	shr̀jǎng	N: mayor	13
市價	shr̀jyà	N: the market price	13

5 （一）

平安	píngān	SV: be peaceful	2
可	kě	A: indeed	9
可惜	kěsyī	MA/SV: too bad/be pitiful	12
可不是嗎	kěbúshr̀ ma	IE: sure enough	15
世	shr̀	BF: world	7
世界	shr̀jyè	N: the world	7
打電報	dǎ dyànbàu	VO: send a telegram	2
打球	dǎchyǒu	VO: play ball	11

石	shŕ	BF:	stone, rock	11
石頭	shŕtou	N:	stone, rock	11
布	bù	N:	cotton cloth	4
布鞋	bùsyé	N:	cotton cloth shoes	4
民	mín	BF:	people	15
民主	mínjǔ	SV:	be democratic	15
民主國家	mínjǔgwójyā	N:	democratic nation	15
司	sz̄	BF:	manage	6
加	jyā	FV:	add, increase	13

5 （丨）

北方	běifāng	PW:	the north	8
北海大學	Běihǎidàsywé	N:	(a fictitious university)	1
目	mù	BF:	eye	15
目的	mùdi	N:	purpose, aim, goal	15
且	chyě	BF:	moreover, furthermore	11
另	lìng	SP:	another	6
另外	lìngwài	SP/MA:	another/besides, in addition	6
史	shǐ	BF:	history	9
只	jǐ	A:	just, only	11
只好	jǐrhǎu	A:	the best thing is to…	11
出租	chūzū	FV:	for rent	5
出產	chūchǎn	N/FV:	products/produce	13
出主意	chū júyi	VO:	suggest a plan	12
以為	yǐwéi	FV:	suppose, think that, take it that	3

5 （丿）

用gūng	yùnggūng	SV:	study hard	10

用力	yùnglì	A:	hard, make an effort	12
生活	shēnghwó	N/V:	livelihood, living/live	7
外科	wàikē	N:	surgical department	10
冬	dūng	BF:	winter	1
冬天	dūngtyān	TW:	winter	1
包	bāu	FV/M:	wrap/parcel, package, pack(of cigaretts)	3, 8
皮	pí	N:	bark, skin, leather, fur	3
皮包	púbāu	N:	suitcase, briefcase, small handbag	3
皮鞋	písyé	N:	leather shoes	4

6 (、)

安	ān	BF:	peace	2
安靜	ānjìng	SV:	be quiet	7
交	jyāu	FV:	give to, deliver, pay	9
交通	jyāutūng	N:	communications	12
交給	jyāugǎi	FV:	turn over to	9

6 (一)

式	shr̀	BF:	style, pattern, fashion	4
再	dzài	A:	then	1
再說	dzàishwō	PH:	see about it, talk further	1
地理	dìlǐ	N:	geography	9
地圖	dìtú	N:	map	8
考	kǎu	FV:	examine, test	9
考試	kǎushr̀	FV/N:	examine, test/examination	9
西湖	Syīhú	PW:	West Lake	13
西湖飯dyàn	Shīhúfàndyàn	N:	West Lake Hotel	13

共	gùng	BF: altogether	1
死	sž	FV: die	7
有理	yǒulǐ	SV: be logical, reasonable	15
有興趣	yǒu syìngchyu	SV/VO: be interested in	12
而	ér	BF: but; and	11
而且	érchyě	MA: besides, moreover, in addition	11

6 （丨）

光	gwāng	N: light, ray	10
早就	dzǎujyòu	A: long since, a long while ago	12
同	túng	BF: the same as	11
同事	túngshr̀	VO/N: work at the same kind of work/colleague	11
同情	túngchíng	FV/N: sympathize with/sympathy	11
同意	túngyì	FV: agree, be of the same opinion	11
同學	túngsywé	VO/N: attend the same school/ schoolmate	11
回答	hwéidá	N/FV: answer	9
肉	ròu	N: meat, flesh	12
收	shōu	FV: receive	2
收到	shōudàu	RV: receive	4
收拾	shōushr	FV: clean up; repair, fix	2, 14
收音機	shōuyīnjī	N: （same as 無線電收音機）	14

6 （丿）

合	hé	FV: join	4
合適	héshr̀	SV: be suitable, fit	4
全	chywán	A/SV: all, entirely/be complete	14

年青	nyánchīng	SV:	be young	12
成	chéng	SV/V/RVE:	be o.k., satisfactory/ become/change into	4, 11
各	gè	SP:	each, every, all	13
各人	gèrén	N:	every person	13
各省	gèshǎng	N:	every province	14
各處	gèchù	PW:	everywhere	13
各種各樣	gèjǔnggèyàng	PH:	every kind	13
多半兒	dwōbàr	A:	the majority, most of	4
多久	dwójyǒu	A-SV:	how long(time)	5
多好幾倍	dwō hǎujǐbèi	PH:	be several times more	15
危	wēi		dangerous	15
危險	wēisyǎn	N/SV:	danger/be dangerous, critical	15
色	sè	BF:	color	4
休	syōu	BF:	rest	8
休息	syōusyi	N/FV:	rest	8
向	syàng	BF:	toward, hitherto	14
向來	syànglái	MA:	hitherto, always	14
行李	syíngli	N:	baggage	2
好像	hǎusyàng	MA:	as though, it seems that	7
好處	hǎuchu	N:	good point, benefit	11
好是好	hǎu shr hǎu	PH:	it is good all right, ...	7
好好兒的	hǎuhāurde	A:	nicely, in a decent manner	10
如	rú	BF:	be like, as,	11

7 (、)

| 決 | jywé | BF: | decide | 5 |
| 決定 | jywéding | FV: | decide | 5 |

沒有關係	*méiyou gwānsyi*	PH:	it doesn't matter	5
汽	*chì*	BF:	steam	3
汽車	*chìchē*	N:	automobile, car	3
汽油	*chìyóu*	N:	gasoline	14
完全	*wánchywán*	A/SV:	completely/be complete	14
究	*jyōu*	BF:	examine into	7
冷	*lěng*	SV:	be cold	8
言	*yán*	BF:	language	14

7 (一)

那麼	*nèmme*	A:	in that case	9
形	*syíng*	BF:	figure, form	9
走過去	*dzǒu gwòchyu*	RV:	go(over)there	7
李	*lǐ*	N:	a surname	2
局	*jyú*	BF:	an office	2

7 (丨)

助	*jù*	BF:	aid, help	15
里	*lǐ*	M:	a Chinese li (1/3 mile)	1
別鬧	*byénàu*	PH:	don't make a row	12

7 (丿)

希	*syī*	BF:	hope	3
希望	*syīwàng*	N/FV:	hope	3
坐滿了	*dzwòmǎnle*	RV:	all seats are taken, (the room) is full	7
利	*lì*	BF:	profit, advantage	9
利害	*lìhai*	SV:	be fierce, severe	9
我敢保險	*wǒ gǎn bǎusyǎn*	PH:	I can be sure, I dare to guarantee	9

我 ywè 想 ywè 學得...	wǒ ywè syǎng ywéde...	PAT:	the more I think, the more I feel...	15
私	sz̄	BF:	private	10
私立	sz̄lì	AT:	privately established (such as school)	10
住校	jùsyàu	VO:	live in the school	8
何	hé	BF:	what? how? why? which?	9
何必	hébì	A:	what need? why must?	9
何必非...不可	hébì fēi...bùkě	PAT:	why insist on....	9
作禮拜	dzwò lǐbài	VO:	go to church	7
低	dī	SV/FV:	be low/lower, bow	7
低頭	dītóu	VO:	bow the head	7
身	shēn	BF:	the body	11
身體	shēntǐ	N:	body; health	11

8 （、）

注	jù	BF:	pay attention	13
注意	jùyì	VO/AV/FV:	pay attention (to)	13
油	yóu	N:	oil; sauce	14
定	dìng	FV:	reserve, subscribe (as a magazine)	1
空	kūng	SV:	be empty, vacant	2
空軍	kūngjyūn	N:	air force	15
空軍基地	kūngjyūnjīdì	N:	air bace	15
放假	fàngjyà	VO:	close school for a vacation	8
房東	fángdūng	N:	landlord, landlady	5
房間	fángjyān	N:	room	5
房租	fángdzū	N:	house rent	5
府	fǔ	BF:	mansion	13

並	*bìng*	BF:	and; also	11
並且	*bìngchyě*	MA:	moreover	11
社	*shè*	BF:	society	9
社會學	*shèhwèisywé*	N:	sociology	9

8 (一)

青	*chīng*	SV:	be blue	12
青年	*chīngnyán*	N:	young person	12
取	*chyǔ*	FV:	fetch (things), take out	6
或	*hwò*	BF:	either, or	13
或是...或是...	*hwòshr...hwòshr*	MA:	either...or...	13
雨	*yǔ*	N:	rain	10
拉	*lā*	FV:	pull	12
到處	*dàuchù*	N:	everywhere	11

8 (丨)

長的	*jǎngde*	FV:	grow	6
非	*fēi*	BF:	be not	3
非常	*fēicháng*	A:	very, extraordinarily	3
花	*hwā*	N:	flower	11
花園子	*hwāywándz*	N:	flower garden	11
門	*mén*	M:	(for courses)	9
門口	*ménkǒu*	PW:	gateway, doorway	13
味	*wèi*	BF:	flavor, taste; smell	10
味兒	*wèr*	N:	taste; odor; aroma	10

8 (丿)

金	*jīn*	BF:	gold	6
金子	*jīndz*	N:	gold	6
忽	*hū*	BF:	sudden	12

忽然	hūrán	MA:	suddenly	12
迎	yíng	BF:	go to meet	14
所	swǒ	M:	(for houses)	5
姐	jyě	BF:	older sister	1
姐姐	jyějye	N:	older sister	1
往上一拉	wàng shàng yilā	PH:	to pull up immediately	12

9 (、)

洋	yáng	N:	ocean	15
活	hwó	FV/SV:	live/be alive	7
派	pài	FV:	send(someone to do something)	6
音	yīn	BF:	sound	5
計	jì	BF:	reckon	13
計劃	jìhwa	N/FV:	plan	13
度	dù	M:	degree	10
軍	jyūn	BF:	military	15
美金	Měijīn	N:	American money (gold)	6
美國式	Měigwóshr̀	AT:	American style	14

9 (一)

春	chwūn	BF:	spring (season)	1
春天	chwūntyan	TW:	spring	1
春假	chwūnjyà	N:	spring vacation	9
封	fēng	M:	(for letters)	1
政	jèng	BF:	administration	13
政府	jèngfŭ	N:	the government, the administration	13
南方	nánfāng	PW:	the south	8
故	gù	BF:	old, ancient	7

故事	gùshr	N:	story	7
按	àn	CV:	according to	5
按月算	àn ywà swàn	PH:	calculate according to month	5
拾	shŕ	FV:	pick up	2
相	syāng	BF:	mutual	12
相當	syāngdāng	A:	fairly	12
查	chá	FV:	investigate	10
查病	chábìng	VO:	be examined for a disease	10
研	yán	BF:	research	7
研究	yánjyōu	N/FV:	reasearch, study	7
架	jyà	M:	(for airplane)	15
降	jyàng	BF:	descend	15
降落	jyànglwò	FV:	land (from the air)	15
飛	fēi	FV:	fly	3
飛機	fēijī	N:	airplane	3
飛行員	fēisyíngywán	N:	flier, aviator	15
飛機塲	fēijīchǎng	N:	airfield, airport	11

9 (丨)

省	shěng	N:	province	8
苦	kǔ	SV:	be bitter to taste; be hard (of life)	7
英	Yīng	BF:	England	9
英文	Yīngwén	N:	English language	9
星	syīng	N:	star	7
星期日	syīngchìr	N:	Sunday	7
界	jyè	BF:	boundary	7

9 （丿）

重	*jùng*	SV:	be heavy	12
重要	*jùngyau*	SV:	be important	12
科	*kē*	N/BF:	department/science	10
科學	*kēsywé*	N:	science	10
科學家	*kēsywéjyā*	N:	scientist	10
秋	*chyōu*	BF:	autumn	1
秋天	*chyōutyan*	TW:	autumn	1
香	*syāng*	SV:	be fragrant, smell good	14
急	*jí*	SV:	be anxious; hurried	3
風	*fēng*	N:	wind	2, 10
風俗	*fēngsú*	N:	custom	14
風景	*fēngjǐng*	N:	scenery, view	2
信	*syìn*	FV:	believe	7
信敎	*syìnjyàu*	VO:	have religion; be a Christian	7
信封	*syìnfēng*	N:	envelope	1
信 jīdū敎	*syìn jīdūjyàu*	VO:	be a Christian	7
保	*bǎu*	BF:	protect	6
保險	*bǎusyǎn*	VO:	take insurance	6
保險公司	*bǎusyǎn gūngsz̄*	N:	insurance company	6
俗	*sú*	SV:	be vulgar; common	14
俗話	*súhwà*	N:	common saying	14
俄	*È*	BF:	Russia	9
俄文	*Èwén*	N:	Russian language	9
係	*syì*	BF:	belong to	5
紅	*húng*	SV:	be red	4

紅銅	húngtúng	N:	copper	10
約	ywē	FV/BF:	invite/agreement	7
約會	ywēhwèi	N:	engagement	7

10 (、)

消	syāu	BF:	diminish	15
消息	syāusyi	N:	news, information	15
海	hǎi	N:	sea	1
海軍	hǎijyūn	N:	navy	15
害	hài	BF:	harm, disadvantage	9
....家	....jyā	BF:	(indicate a specialist)	10
記	jì	FV:	remember, recollect	3
記得	jide	FV:	remember	3
病人	bìngren	N:	patient	10
旅	lyǔ	BF:	travel	2
旅行	lyǔsyíng	N/FV:	trip/travel	2
旅館	lyǔgwǎn	N:	hotel	2
旅行團	lyǔsyíngtwán	N:	travel club	13
高興	gāusyìng	SV:	be happy	7
神	shén	N:	spirit; deity, God	11
烟	yān	N:	tobacco; cigarette; smoke	5

10 (一)

起飛	chǐfēi	FV:	take off (airplane)	3
恐	kǔng	BF:	afraid	2
恐怕	kǔngpà	MA:	perhaps, probably	2
夏	syà	BF:	summer	1
夏天	syàtyan	TW:	summer	1
原	ywán	BF:	origin, reason, cause	10

原來	ywánlái	MA: originally	11
原故	ywángù	N: reason, cause	10
院	ywàn	BF: courtyard, hall; institute	10
除	chú	BF: deduct	6
除了…以外	chúle…yǐwài	PAT: in addition to…, besides; except	6

0（丨）

草	tsǎu	N: grass	8
草地	tsǎudì	N: lawn	8
茶葉	cháyè	N: tea leaves	13
剛	gāng	A: just this minute	1
剛才	gāngtsái	MA: just a moment ago	1
時間	shŕjyān	N: time, period	2
員	ywán	BF: personnel	15

10（丿）

特	tè	BF: special	2
特別	tèbyé	SV/A: be special/especially	2
特別快車	tèbyékwàichē	N: express train	3
租	bzū	FV: rent	5
租給	dzūgěi	FV: rent (it) to	5
倍	bèi	M: time. -fold	13
隻	jī	M: (for animal, birds, etc.)	12
借	jyè	FV: borrow, lend	9
值	jŕ	FV: be worth (so much)	6
值得	jŕde	SV: be worthwhile	10
值錢	jŕchyán	VO/SV: be worth (so much) money/be valuable	6

息	*syī*	BF:	rest	8
留	*lyóu*	FV:	keep; detain; leave	5
留學	*lyóusywé*	FV:	study abroad	5
留定錢	*lyóu dìngchyan*	VO:	leave a deposit	5
留兩天	*lyóu lyǎngtyān*	PH:	keep for two days	5
航	*háng*	BF:	sail, navigate	2
航空	*hángkūng*	BF:	aviation	2
航空信	*hángkūngsyìn*	N:	air mail	2

11 (ﾍ)

涼	*lyáng*	SV:	be cool, cold	8
涼快	*lyángkwài*	SV:	be cool	8
深	*shēn*	SV:	be deep (color, water, thought)	4
清	*chīng*	BF:	be clear	3
清楚	*chīngchu*	SV:	be clear	3
清算	*chīngswàn*	FV:	liquidate	15
淺	*chyǎn*	SV:	be light (in color); shallow (of water, thought)	4
淺黃	*chyǎnhwáng*	N:	light yellow	4
淨	*jìng*	BF:	clean	2
寄	*jì*	FV:	mail, send by mail	2
寄走了	*jìdzǒule*	RV:	mailed out	4
部	*bù*	M:	part, section	15
商	*shāng*	BF:	trade, commerce; discuss	4
商人	*shāngren*	N:	a merchant	4
商量	*shānglyang*	FV:	discuss, talk over	4
情形	*chíngsying*	N:	condition, situation	9

惜	syī	BF: pity	12
望	wàng	BF: hope, expect	3
產	chǎn	FV: produce	13

11 (一)

雪	sywě	N: snow	8
通	tūng	BF: all, universal	12
球	chyóu	N: ball	11
理	lǐ	N: reason	7
規	gwēi	BF: custom, usage, regulation	8
規定	gwēidìng	FV: regulate	8
救	jyòu	FV: save, rescue	15
連	lyán	CV: even	9
連...都...	lyán...dōu...	PAT: even...	9
教堂	jyàutáng	N: church (building)	7
票	pyàu	N: ticket	3
票房	pyàufáng	N: ticket office	3
基	jī	BF: base	15
基地	jīdì	N: base	15
乾	gān	SV: be dry	2
乾淨	gānjing	SV: be clean	2
接	jyē	FV: receive, meet (at a train, boat, etc.)	1
接着	jyējáu	RV: received, met	1
接着	jyēje	A: continue, go on	5
接電話	jyē dyànhwà	VO: answer a phone call	8
推	twēi	FV: push	12
推不動	twēi budùng	RV: not able to move (by pushing)	14

推了他一下	*twèile tā yisyà*	PH:	gave him a push	12
習	*syí*	BF:	practice, learn	9
習慣	*syígwàn*	N:	habit	14
蛋	*dàn*	N:	egg	12
陸	*lù*	BF:	land	15
陸軍	*lùjyūn*	N:	army	15
研	*yán*	BF:	research	7
研究	*yánjyou*	N/FV:	research, study	7

11 （丨）

堂	*táng*	BF:	hall, room	7
處	*chù*	BF:	place, point	11
畢	*bì*	BF:	finish	1
畢業	*bìyè*	VO:	graduate	1
問題	*wènti*	N:	question, problem	9
國民	*gwómín*	N:	national, people	15
國語	*gwóyǔ*	N:	the Chinese national language, Mandarin	3
將	*jyāng*	BF:	about to	14
將來	*jyānglái*	MA:	in the future	14

11 （丿）

動	*dùng*	FV:	move; wiggle	8, 12
動身	*dùngshēn*	VO:	start (on a journey)	11
動員	*dùngywán*	FV:	mobilize	15
鳥	*nyǎu*	N:	bird	8
鳥兒叫	*nyǎur jyàu*	PH:	singing of birds	8
停	*tíng*	FV:	stop	3
既	*jì*	BF:	since	11

旣然	jìrán	MA:	since it is so	11
假	jyà	N:	vacation, leave of absence	8
偷	tōu	FV:	steal	6
偷偷的	tōutōude	A:	stealthily, secretly	6
參	tsān	BF:	participate in	8
參加	tsānjyā	FV:	participate in, join	13
參觀	tsāngwān	FV:	pay a visit to (a public place)	8
參考書	tsānkǎuʂhū	N:	a reference book	9
婚	hwūn	BF:	marriage	5
紹	shàu	BF:	connect, join	1
組	dzǔ	BF:	organize	13
組織	dzǔjŕ	N/FV:	organization/organize	13

12 (、)

湖	hú	N:	lake	11
湖邊兒	húbyār	PW:	lake shore, lake side	11
溫	wēn	SV:	be warm	10
溫度	wēndù	N:	temperature	10
痛	tùng	SV:	be painful	10
普	pǔ	BF:	general	12
普通	pǔtūng	SV:	be general, common	12
着急	jāují	SV:	be worried, get excited	3
着涼	jāulyáng	VO:	catch cold	8

12 (一)

替	tì	CV:	for (in place of)	2
敢	gǎn	AV:	dare, venture	6
期	chī	BF:	period, date	7

換	hwàn	FV:	exchange, change	4
發	fā	BF:	start; grow; put forth	10
發明	fāmíng	FV:	invent	10
發現	fāsyàn	FV:	discover	10
發燒	fāshāu	VO:	have a fever	10
費	fei	FV:	waste; use a lot	9
費錢	feichyán	VO/SV:	cost money, waste money/ be expensive	9
黃	hwáng	SV:	be yellow	4
陽	yáng	BF:	sun	11

12 (丨)

黑市	hēishr̀	N:	black market	13
黑bǎn	hēibǎn	N:	black board	9
景	jǐng	BF:	scenery, view	2
量	lyáng	FV:	measure	4
	lyàng	BF:	deliberate	4
間	jyān	M/BF:	(for room)/space between	2
開燈	kāidēng	VO:	turn on lights	5
開學	kāisywé	VO:	school starts	9
開單子	kāidāndz	VO:	make out a list	6
開玩笑	kāiwásyàu	VO:	make fun of	12
單	dān	BF:	simple	5
單子	dāndz	N:	list	6
貴的不貴 jyàn的不jyàn	gwèide búgwèi jyànde bújyàn	PH:	"Expensive things are (in the end) not expensive, (while) cheap ones are (really) not cheap."	4
過去了	gwòchyule	RV:	passed away	7
過 (NuM) 街	gwò(NuM)jyē	PH:	go (Nu) blocks	8

12 （丿）

答	dá	FV: answer, reply	9
郵	yóu	BF: postal	2
郵局	yóujyú	N: post office	2
無	wú	BF: wihout, none	14
無論	wúlwùn	A: no matter what..., it doesn't matter...	14
無線電	wúsyàndyàn	N: (Same as 無線電收音機)	14
無線電收音機	wúsyàndyàn shōuyīnjī	N: radio receiving set	14
備	bèi	BF: prepare	1
結	jyé	BF: unite, connect	5
結婚	jyéhwūn	VO: get married; marriage	5
結實	jyēshr	SV: be strong	6
鄉	syāng	BF: the country	1
鄉下	syāngsya	PW: rural district, country	1

13 （、）

新式	syīnshr̀	SV: be modern	4
該	gāi	AV: ought, should	6
該我了	gāi wǒ le	PH: now it is my turn	10
試	shr̀	FV: try	4
試試	shr̀shr̀	FV: try	4
誠	chéng	BF: honest, sincere	12
誠實	chéngshr̀	SV: be honest, sincere	12
運	yùn	BF: move around	8
運氣	yùnchi	N: luck, fortune	14
運動	yùndung	N/FV: sports; physical exercise/ take physical exercise	8

運動會	*yùndùnghwèi*	N:	athletic meeting	8
運動場	*yùndùngchǎng*	N:	athletic field	8
道理	*dàuli*	N:	teaching, doctrine	7

13 (一)

電	*dyàn*	N:	electricity	2
電車	*dyànchē*	N:	trolley car	2
電話	*dyànhwà*	N:	telephone	3
電報	*dyànbàu*	N:	telegram, cable	2
電燈	*dyàndēng*	N:	electric light	5
電影	*dyànyǐng*	N:	motion picture	11
電影院	*dyànyǐngywàn*	N:	movie theater	11
電報局	*dyànbàujyú*	N:	telegraph office	2
零	*líng*	NU:	zero	3
較	*jyǎu*	BF:	compare	14
楚	*chǔ*	BF:	clear, distinct	3
預	*yù*	BF:	prepare	1
預先	*yùsyān*	A:	beforehand	1
預定	*yùdìng*	FV:	order or subscribe; reserve	1
預備	*yùbei*	FV:	prepare	1

13 (|)

落	*lwò*	FV:	come down	15
葉	*yè*	BF:	leaf	13
嗎	*ma*	P :	(question particle)	6
賊	*dzéi*	N:	thief	6
照	*jàu*	FV:	reflect	10
照像	*jàusyàng*	VO:	take photographs	10

照照像	jàujàusyàng	VO:	take photographs(the duplication of functive verbs indicates casualness)	10
照 X 光	jàu àikeszgwāng	VO:	take an X-ray picture	10
號	hàu	M:	size; day(of month), number (of house, telephone, etc.)	4
園	ywán	BF:	garden, park	11
跟着	gēnje	CV:	follow	7
跟着唱	gēnje chàng	PH:	to sing after (people)	7
業	ye	BF:	profession; business	1
裝	jwāng	FV:	pack, load	14

13 (丿)

會	hwèi	AV:	may, would	2
解	jyě	FV:	loosen, untie	13
解決	jyějywé	FV:	solve	13
解放	jyěfàng	FV:	emancipate, liberate	15
經濟	jīngjì	N:	economics	14

14 (丶)

滿	mǎn	SV:	be full	7
實	shŕ	BF:	real, solid	6
實在	shŕdzài	SV/A:	be real, honest / really, actually	6
察	chá	BF:	find out	6
誌	jr̀	BF:	record	15
語	yǔ	BF:	language; a set phrase	3
語言	yǔyán	N:	language	14
慢慢兒的	mànmānrde	A:	slowly	6
慣	gwàn	SV:	be accustomed	14

精	*jīng*	BF:	spirit, essence	11
精神	*jīngshén*	N:	spirit, spiritual part of man	11

14 (一)

需	*syū*	BF:	need	5
需要	*syūyàu*	N/FV:	need	5
劃	*hwà*	BF:	plan	13
輕	*chīng*	SV:	be light (in weight)	14
場	*chǎng*	BF:	field	8

14 (丨)

圖	*tú*	N:	picture, map, diagram	8
圖書館	*túshūgwǎn*	N:	library	8
團	*twán*	BF:	corps, club	13
對…有研究	*dwèi…yǒuyánjyōu*	PAT:	have specialized knowledge in…	7

14 (丿)

銀	*yín*	BF:	silver	6
銀行	*yínháng*	N:	bank	6
銅	*túng*	N:	copper, brass	6
管	*gwǎn*	FV:	manage; take care, attend to	5
管燈水	*gwǎn dāngshwěi*	PH:	including electricity and water	5
算了吧	*swànle ba*	PH:	let's forget it, let's drop the matter	7
種	*jǔng*	M:	kind, species	8
種類	*jǔnglèi*	N:	kind, species	14
像	*syàng*	SV:	be like; resemble	5
綠	*lyù*	SV:	be green	8

15 （、）

窮	chyúng	SV:	be poor	7
窮得沒飯吃	chyúngde méifàn- chr̄	PH:	(He was) so poor that (he) could not afford food	7
適	shr̀	BF:	be suitable, fit	4
談	tán	FV:	chat, talk about	1
談話	tánhwà	VO:	carry on conversation	1
課	kè	M/N:	(for lessons)/school work	8
課堂	kètáng	N:	classroom	8
論	lwùn	BF:	discuss, speak of	14
熟	shú	SV:	be very familiar	13
廣	gwǎng	SV:	be broad	5
廣告	gwǎnggàu	N:	advertisement	5
廣東省	Gwǎngdūngshěng	PW:	Kwangtung Province	9

15 （一）

趣	chyù	BF:	interest	12
熱	rè	SV:	be hot	2
熱心	rèsyīn	SV:	be zealous, enthusiastic	2
熱鬧	rènau	SV:	be bustling, lively	12
暫	jàn	BF:	temporarily	5
暫時	jànshŕ	MA:	temporarily	5
鞋	syé	N:	shoe	4
樓	lóu	N/M:	storied building/ (for floors)	4
概	gài	BF:	in general	1

15 （｜）

鬧	nàu	FV/SV:	make disturbance/ be noisy	12

影	*yǐng*	BF:	shadow, image, reflection	11

15 (丿)

價	*jyà*	BF:	price, cost	4
價錢	*jyàchyan*	N:	price, cost	4
德	*Dé*	BF:	Germany; virtue	4
德國	*Dégwó*	PW:	Germany	4
練	*lyàn*	FV:	practice	9
練習	*lyànsyí*	N/FV:	practice; exercise/ practice	9
線	*syàn*	N:	line; wire	14

16 (丶)

燒	*shāu*	FV:	burn	10
燈	*deng*	N:	lamp, light	5

16 (一)

靜	*jìng*	SV:	be quiet	7
頭痛	*tóutùng*	SV:	have a headache	10
據	*jyù*	CV:	according to	15
據說	*jyùshwō*	IE:	it is said, it is reported	15
樹	*shù*	N:	tree	8
機	*jī*	BF:	opportune; machine	3
機會	*jīhwèi*	N:	opportunity, chance	3
機器	*jīchì*	N:	machine, engine	14
歷	*lì*	BF:	pass through	9
歷史	*lìshǐ*	N:	history	9
險	*syǎn*	BF:	danger	6
隨	*swéi*	BF:	follow	10
隨便	*swéibyàn*	A/SV:	do as one pleases/be casual; unconcerned	10

隨時	swéishŕ	A:	at all times, at any moment	10

16（丨）

縣	syàn	N/M:	distrit, *hsien*	13
器	chì	BF:	tool	14

16（丿）

錯兒	tswòr	N:	fault, mistake	6
舉	jyǔ	V:	raise	9
舉手	jyǔshǒu	VO:	raise one's hand	9
興	syìng	BF:	interest, excitement	7

17（、）

濟	jì	BF:	aid	14
講	jyǎng	FV:	explain, talk	7
講話	jyǎnghwà	VO:	talk	13
講書	jyǎngshū	VO:	explain the lesson	9
講道	jyǎngdàu	VO:	preach	7
應該	yīnggāi	AV:	should, ought	6

17（一）

幫助	bāngjù	N/FV:	help	15
聲	shēng	BF:	sound; voice	5
聲音	shēngyin	N:	voice; noise; sound	5
聯	lyán	BF:	unite	15
聯合國	Lyánhégwó	N:	The United Nations	15
檢	jyǎn	BF:	examine	10
檢查	jyǎnchá	FV:	examine	10

17（丨）

雖	swéi	BF:	although	5

雖然	*swéirán*	A:	although	5
牆	*chyáng*	N:	wall	5
戲	*syì*	N:	play, opera	11

17 (|)

| 總(是) | *dzǔng(shr)* | A: | always, in every case | 9 |

18 (、)

顏	*yán*	BF:	color	4
顏色	*yánsè*	N:	color	4
讓	*ràng*	CV:	(indicates agent) by; let, allow	3
護	*hù*	BF:	protect, guard	10
護士	*hùshr*	N:	nurse	10
懶	*lǎn*	SV:	be lazy	12
雜	*dzá*	BF:	miscallaneous	15
雜誌	*dzájr*	N:	magazine	15
離婚	*líhwūn*	VO:	divorce	5
類	*lèi*	M:	category	14

18 (一)

聽戲	*tīngsyi*	VO:	go to a play	11
醫	*yī*	BF:	heal, cure; a doctor	10
醫生	*yīshēn*	N:	doctor	10
醫院	*yīywàn*	N:	hospital, dispensary	10

18 (|)

觀	*gwān*	BF:	see, look at	8
歡迎	*hwānyíng*	FV:	welcome	14
蘇	*Sū*	BF:	Soviet Union	15
蘇聯	*Sūlyán*	N:	Soviet Union	15

警	jǐng	BF:	warn, caution	6
警告	jǐnggàu	N/FV:	warning/warn	6
警察	jǐngchá	N:	policeman	6
警察局	jǐngchájyú	N:	police department	6
舊式	jyòushr	SV:	be old fashioned	6
藥	yàu	N:	medicine, drug; herb	10
題	tí	BF:	theme, subject	9
關係	gwānsyi	N:	relation	5
關 yu	gwānyu	CV:	about, concerning	14
體	tǐ	BF:	the body	11

18 (丿)

雞	jī	N:	chicken	12
雞蛋	jīdàn	N:	(chicken)egg	12
鐵	tyě	N:	iron	13
鐵路	tyělù	N:	a railway	13
簡	jyǎn	BF:	be simple	3
簡直	jyǎnjŕ	A:	simply	3
簡單	jyǎndān	SV:	be simple	5
織	jŕ	FV:	weave(cloth, etc.)	13

C chídǎu		FV:	pray	7
chōu 烟	chōuyān	VO:	smoke	5
D dyàu 魚	dyàuyú	VO:	fish	12
dyàu 下去	dyàusyachyu	RV:	drop, fall	12
dyōu 了	dyōule	FV:	lost	7

	dzàn 美shr̄	*dzànměishr̄*	N:	hymn	7
	dzwò 位	*dzwòwei*	N:	seat	7
G	gǎi 成	*gǎichéng*	RV:	change into	13
	gǎn 緊	*gǎnjǐn*	A:	hurriedly, at once	13
	gūng 課	*gūngkè*	N:	school work	10
	gūng 課 表	*gūngkèbyǎu*	N:	schedule (of day's classes)	9
H	Hángjōu 市	*Hángjōushr̀*	PW:	city of Hangchow	13
	hé 子	*hédz*	N:	box (small)	14
	hwò 是	*hwòshr*	A:	or	9
J	já 雞	*jájī*	N:	fried chicken	14
	jyǎu		N:	foot	4
L	lyàng		M:	(for cars)	12
	lyǔ 館	*lyǔgwǎn*	N:	hotel	1
M	mùshr		N:	pastor, minister	7
N	nèi 科	*nèikē*	N:	medical department	10
	nùng 錯 子	*nùngtswòle*	PH:	made a mistake	3
S	shwāng	*sùshè*	M:	pair (for shoes, socks, etc)	4
	sùshè		N:	dormitory	8
	syāng 子	*syāngdz*	N:	suitcase; trunk	14
T	tǐyù 館	*tǐyùgwǎn*	N:	gym	8
	túng 學	*túngsywé*	N:	schoolmate	10
	twō		FV:	take off (as clothes)	6
V	V 給	*V gěi*	FV:	V to	5
W	wà 子	*wàdz*	N:	sock, stocking	4
Y	ywè 來 ywè SV	*ywèláiywè SV*	PAT:	getting SV-er and SV-er	9

NUMBER OF STROKES AND STROKE ORDER LIST OF THE
300 BASIC CHINESE CHARACTERS INTRODUCED IN THIS BOOK

In writing Chinese characters, it is important to observe certain principles of stroke order evolved from the experience of many generations of Chinese calligraphers. Important as they are, these principles are very general in nature and people do differ in minor details. Just as many an American would say, 'Nobody is going to tell me whether to write the horizontal or the vertical line first in the capital letter T,' the Chinese people can be equally stubborn in this matter. Listed below are seven of the most generally observed principles.

1. From upper left-hand corner to lower right-hand corner. This is an over-all principle, embracing the remaining six, and guides the writing of all characters not covered by them (see illustrations 1 to 6).
2. From left to right, as in ╱╲ (see illustration 1).
3. From top to bottom, as in ⚏ (see illustration 2).
4. From outside to inside, as in 日 (see illustration 3). Note how the inside is filled in first before the base line is added.
5. Horizontal before other lines crossing it, as in ┼ (see illustration 4).
6. Slanting stroke to the left before the one to the right, as in ㄨ (see illustration 5).
7. Center stroke before its symmetrical wings, as in ⺌ (see illustration 6).

	ILLUSTRATION	STROKE ORDER			
1	╱╲	╱	╱╲		
2	⚏	⚊	⚏		
3	日	⎮	⺆	⺆	日
4	┼	⚊	┼		
5	父	╱	⺀	⺁	父
6	⺌	⎨	⺀	⺌	

Supplementary illustrations to show the Principles of stroke order, and direction of each stroke.

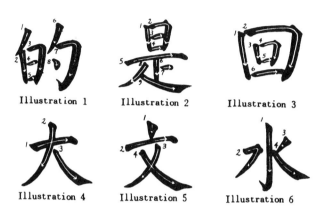

Illustration 1   Illustration 2   Illustration 3

Illustration 4   Illustration 5   Illustration 6

The number of strokes in a certain character sometimes differs from one writer to another, and even from one dictionary to another. In debatable cases, arbitrary determination of the number of strokes, based on common usage, has been made by the author in order to avoid unnecessary problems for the beginning student.

In the following list, if the written form differs from the printed form, the former is used.

Chinese calligraphy is an art in itself, comparable to Chinese painting in importance and artistic expression, and requiring much practice to achieve perfection. What can be briefly mentioned here is that characters should be as square and proportional as possible and the strokes even and vigorous. Chinese character writing is to a considerable extent character expression, and you write what you are.

海	丶	宀	氵	姐	く	女	女
	氵	氵	沪		如	如	如
10 strokes	海	海	海	8	姐	姐	
鄉	ㄥ	ㄠ	纟	冬	丿	ㄱ	夂
	幺	纟	纟		冬	冬	
12 strokes	绅	绅	鄉	5			
概	十	木	朾	畢	口	日	旦
	栌	根	根		旦	旦	旦
13 strokes	柜	概	概	11	畧	畧	畢
里	丶	冂	曰	業	‖	业	业
	日	旦	甲		业	业	业
7 strokes	里			13	業	業	業
共	一	十	卄	春	一	二	三
	廾	共	共		夫	夫	夫
6 strokes				9	春	春	春

夏	一	丆	丆	封	一	十	圡
	万	百	百		圭	丰	圭
10	頁	夏	夏	9	圭	封	封
剛	丨	冂	冈	接	一	扌	扌
	冈	冈	岡		扩	扩	拉
10	岡	剛	剛	11	挨	接	接
秋	丿	二	千	介	丿	人	介
	禾	禾	禾		介		
9	秋	秋	秋	4			
談	亠	言	言	紹	乚	幺	幺
	言	言	訁		糸	紀	紹
15	訁	談	談	11	紹	紹	紹
預	乛	乛	予	備	亻	亻	供
	予	予	予		伊	伊	備
13	預	預	預	12	備	備	備

收	ㄥ	屮	屮	恐	一	ㄟ	工
	屮	屮	收		ㄓ	巩	巩
6				10	巩	恐	恐
拾	一	扌	扌	乾	十	十	古
	扌	扐	抄		古	直	直
8	拾	拾	拾	11	車	乾	乾
李	一	十	才	淨	氵	氵	氵
	木	杢	李		氵	汮	汮
7	李			11	汮	汮	淨
特	丿	牜	牜	間	丨	冂	冂
	牜	牜	牪		冂	門	門
10	牪	特	特	12	門	閂	間
熱	圥	夫	圥	電	一	冖	冖
	坴	坴	埶		雨	雨	雨
15	埶	熱	熱	13	雨	雷	電

局	ㄱ	匚	尸	替	二	丰	夫
	尸	局	局	日	扗	扙	扙
7	局			12	替	替	替
寄	丶	宀	宀	風	丿	几	凡
	宀	宋	宊		凡	同	同
11	室	害	寄	9	風	風	風
航	丶	亻	亻	景	丶	口	日
	舟	舟	舟		旦	旦	旱
10	舟	航	航	12	景	景	景
空	丶	八	宀	旅	二	亠	方
	宀	穴	空		方	扐	扙
8	空	空		10	旅	旅	旅
安	丶	丶	宀	郵	二	亠	亠
	宀	安	安		扐	垂	垂
6				12	垂	郵	郵

記	、	亠	言	楚	一	十	木
	言	言	言		杧	林	埜
10	訂	訂	記	13	埜	楚	楚
非	丿	ナ	扌	立	、	亠	六
	爿	非	非		立	立	
8	非	非		5			
飛	乁	乁	乁	語	、	亠	言
	飞	飞	飞		言	訂	訂
11	飞	飛	飛	14	話	語	語
機	木	杧	松	讓	言	訇	訇
	棪	機	機		誾	譚	讓
16	機	機	機	24	讓	讓	讓
清	氵	氵	汁	急	丿	夕	多
	汁	沣	清		多	多	急
11	清	清	清	9	急	急	急

簡	⺮	⺮	⺮	包	⺀	⺆	勹
	節	節	簡		勹	包	
18	簡	簡	簡	5			
午	⼃	⺊	⺦	汽	⺀	⺀	氵
	午				氵	汁	汽
4				7	汽		
零	⼀	⼆	示	票	⼀	⼂	襾
	示	零	雨		西	西	西
13	零	零	零	11	票	票	票
停	⼂	亻	亻	希	⼃	⼂	⼂
	亻	佇	佇		犭	希	希
11	停	停	停	7	希		
皮	⼃	⼚	⺁	望	⺀	⼃	亡
	皮	皮			切	切	切
5				11	望	望	望

顏	㇒	㇇	产
	彥	彥	顏
18	顏	顏	顏

深	㇒	㇒	沪
	沪	深	深
11	浮	深	深

色	㇒	㇇	㇇
	名	多	色
6			

價	亻	亻	伒
	俪	俪	價
15	價	價	價

布	一	ナ	右
	右	布	
5			

成	一	厂	厉
	成	成	成
6			

鞋	一	廿	廿
	苩	苴	革
15	革	革	鞋

換	扌	扌	扮
	护	护	搞
12	掐	換	換

黃	廿	廿	芏
	芇	苦	苗
12	苗	黃	黃

式	一	二	干
	王	式	式
6			

樓	木 木㭂	杧 柟	杧 楫	適	一 㡿 啇	亠 南 啇 滴	宀 商 適
15	楒	樓	樓	14	滴	滴	適
德	⺅ ⾏	彳 德	彳 德	紅	ㄥ 糸	幺 糸	幺 糸
15	德	德	德	9	紅	紅	紅
淺	氵 淺	氵 淺	汁 淺	號	口 号	旦 号	号 号
11	淺	淺	淺	13	号虎	號	號
試	丶 計	言 訐	言 訐	商	丶 商	一 商	亠 商
13	訐	試	試	11	商	商	商
合	丿 亼	人 合	亼 合	量	口 旦	曰 昌	曰 昌
6				12	量	量	量

租	´	二	千	單	口	口	吅
	禾	禾	利		吅	罒	甲
10	利	租	租	12	甲	單	單
廣	亠	广	广	按	一	寸	才
	庐	庶	庶		扌	扩	护
15	廥	廣	廣	9	拧	按	按
結	乙	幺	幺	管	ノ	𠂉	𥫗
	糸	紅	紝		竹	竺	竺
12	紝	結	結	14	笁	筦	管
婚	𡿨	女	女	燈	火	炒	灯
	妒	妗	娇		炒	炊	烊
11	娇	婚	婚	16	熔	燈	燈
雖	口	吕	吊	烟	丷	少	火
	虽	虽	虽		灯	炉	炯
17	蚩	雖	雖	10	烟	烟	烟

係	ノ	イ	亻'	留	ノ	亠	幻
	亻'	亻'	亻'		幻	切	窗
9	係	係	係	10	留	留	留
聲	一	士	声	像	イ	亻'	亻'
	声	殸	殸		俦	伢	像
17	殸	聲	聲	14	像	像	像
音	丶	亠	六	久	ノ	ク	久
	六	立	产				
9	音	音	音	3			
暫	一	冂	百	需	一	二	干
	亘	車	斬		雨	雨	雨
15	斬	暫	暫	14	雫	雳	需
決	丶	氵	氵	牆	㇄	爿	爿
	氵	江	決		牀	牀	牀
7	決			17	牆	牆	牆

偷	亻	亻	亻	派	丶	冫	氵
	伶	价	价		汀	汋	泝
11	偷	偷	偷	9	派	派	派
賊	丨	冂	目	銀	人	仐	牟
	貝	貝	貯		金	釘	釘
13	賦	賊	賊	14	鈤	銀	銀
寶	丶	宀	宀	取	一	厂	厂
	宀	安	安		耳	耳	耳
14	宵	寶	寶	8	取	取	
警	丷	艹	芍	金	丿	人	仐
	苟	敬	敬		仐	仝	余
20	警	警	警	8	余	金	
察	宀	宀	宀	除	乛	阝	阝
	宀	宀	宀		阝	队	阶
14	宓	察	察	10	除	除	除

另	丶	口	口	該	亠	言	言
	弓	另			言	計	訢
5				13	該	該	該
值	亻	仁	仕	敢	一	丆	工
	忙	佔	佔		丆	音	亘
10	值	值	值	12	耳	敢	敢
銅	人	今	全	公	丿	八	公
	金	金	釗		公		
14	銅	銅	銅	4			
保	丿	亻	伫	司	乛	刁	司
	伫	伫	但		司	司	
9	伃	伊	保	5			
險	阝	阝	阶	嗎	丶	口	口
	阶	险	险		吖	吗	呼
16	险	险	險	13	哗	嗎	嗎

星	丨	冂	日	興	亻	𠂉	𠂤
9	日	尸	早	16	铜	铜	铜
	星	星	星		铜	铜	興
期	一	十	卄	研	厂	丆	石
12	甘	其	其	11	石	石	石
	其	期	期		研	研	研
堂	丶	丷	丳	究	丶	宀	宀
11	丷	尚	尚	7	宀	穴	穴
	堂	堂	堂		究		
世	一	十	卄	理	一	二	千
5	世	世		11	王	玑	珇
					珇	理	理
界	丶	冂	日	講	丶	言	言
9	用	田	界	17	言	講	講
	界	界	界		講	講	講

約	㇑	㇑	㇑	故	一	十	十
	糸	糸	糸		古	古	古
9	糸	約	約	9	故	故	故
反	㇒	㇒	厂	窮	宀	穴	穴
	反				穷	宵	穿
4				15	窘	窮	窮
滿	氵	氵	汁	苦	丶	艹	艹
	汁	沣	满		艹	屮	丗
14	满	滿	滿	9	芓	苦	苦
靜	二	丰	圭	死	一	厂	歹
	青	青	靜		歹	歹	死
16	靜	靜	靜	6			
低	㇒	亻	亻	活	丶	冫	氵
	�乐	仾	低		氵	汢	汗
7	低			9	汗	活	活

課	丶	言	言	息	丿	亻	勹
	訶	評	評		自	自	自
15	課	課	課	10	息	息	息
參	㇛	厶	台	綠	幺	糸	糸
	台	幺	灸		糸	絲	綠
11	灸	參	參	14	綠	綠	綠
觀	卄	苗	莭	草	丁	丬	卄
	萑	莋	雚		艹	节	苩
25	雚	觀	觀	10	苩	莗	草
涼	丶	冫	氵	樹	十	木	杜
	沪	泞	泞		杜	桔	桔
11	涼	涼	涼	16	桔	樹	樹
休	丿	亻	仁	鳥	丿	亻	户
	什	休	休		户	鸟	鳥
6				11	鳥	鳥	鳥

雪	一	一	二	假	亻	亻	亻
	币	雷	雫		伊	假	假
11	雪	雪	雪	11	假	假	假
冷	、	ソ	ソ	運	一	冖	冒
	氿	冷	冷		宣	軍	軍
7	冷			13	渾	渾	運
規	二	扌	夫	動	丶	二	亠
	刦	夫刀	夫刀		台	甶	重
11	規	規	規	11	重	動	動
省	丶	小	小	場	十	土	圠
	少	少	省		坦	坦	坦
9	省	省	省	12	場	場	場
圖	丨	冂	同	種	彳	禾	种
	同	圊	圕		稻	稻	稻
14	圖	圖	圖	14	稻	種	種

歷	一	厂	斥	考	一	十	土
	屏	麻	麻		耂	耂	考
16	歷	歷	歷	6			
史	丶	冂	口	練	乚	幺	幺
	史	史			糸	紅	紅
5				15	綀	練	練
俄	丿	亻	亻	習	刁	刁	习
	仁	仵	仵		羽	羽	羽
9	俄	俄	俄	11	翌	習	習
何	丿	亻	亻	題	日	旦	早
	仁	佰	佰		早	是	是
7	何			18	題	題	題
英	丶	十	艹	連	一	冂	百
	艹	艽	芢		亘	車	車
9	苤	英	英	11	連	連	連

社	、	ブ	ネ	舉	ｌ	乃	彷
	ネ	ネ	社		甸	舁	與
7	社			17	與	舉	舉
利	ノ	ニ	千	答	'	⸍	⸍⸍
	壬	禾	利		竹	竺	笒
7	利			12	答	答	答
害	、	宀	宀	借	イ	亻	什
	宀	宇	宝		什	供	供
10	宝	害	害	10	借	借	借
總	糸	幺	約	交	、	亠	亠
	絢	緫	總		六	交	交
17	緫	總	總	6			
形	一	二	干	費	フ	ㄱ	弓
	开	形	形		弗	弗	費
9	形	形	形	12	費	費	費

味	丶	口	口	私	ノ	ニ	千
	口一	叮二	吽		千	禾	禾
8	咮	味		7	私		
雨	一	一	冂	醫	毛	医	殹
	而	雨	雨		殹	殹	醫
8	雨	雨		18	醫	醫	醫
痛	丶	广	疒	院	⁊	⻖	⻖
	疔	疔	疔		⻖	阼	阼
12	痞	痛	痛	10	院	院	院
發	⁊	⁊	⁊	檢	十	木	木
	癶	癶	癶		朳	枠	检
12	登	發	發	17	椧	檢	檢
燒	火	火	火	查	一	十	才
	灶	焼	燒		木	杧	杳
16	燒	燒	燒	9	杳	杳	查

温	氵	氵	沪	藥	艹	艹	芍
	沪	沪	涃		苩	䓓	蕐
12	涃	湡	温	19	蕐	藥	藥
度	丶	一	广	照	丨	冂	日
	广	庐	庐		日丁	昭	昭
9	庐	庲	度	13	照	照	照
原	一	厂	厂	光	丨	丷	小
	厂	厉	盾		业	米	光
10	盾	原	原	6			
護	艹	言	訁	隨	阝	阝	阼
	䕶	諅	護		阝左	隋	隋
21	護	護	護	16	隨	隨	隨
士	一	十	士	科	丿	二	千
					千	禾	禾
3				9	科	科	科

影	丶	冂	日	且	丨	冂	月
	曰	旦	景		月	且	
15	景	景	影	5			
陽	3	阝	阝口	同	丨	冂	冂
	阳	阻	陥		同	同	同
12	陽	陽	陽	6			
如	く	乂	女	並	丶	丷	丷
	如	如	如		丷	並	並
6				8	並	並	
園	冂	冂	冃	身	丿	亻	勹
	禺	周	園		勹	身	身
13	園	園	園	7	身		
而	一	丁	丆	骨豊	冂	冃	冎
	丙	而	而		骨	骨	骨
6				23	體	體	體

精	丶	丷	半
	米	粎	粄
14	粝	精	精

湖	氵	汇	汁
	汁	沽	沽
12	泏	湖	湖

神	丶	⺀	礻
	礻	衤	初
9	袑	袒	神

戲	丨	卢	虍
	虘	虗	虘
17	戱	戲	戲

處	丨	⺊	上
	庐	虍	虎
11	虏	處	處

球	一	二	干
	王	玉	珒
11	珁	球	球

花	丶	丷	卝
	扗	芴	花
8	花	花	

既	彐	彐	彐
	艮	艮	艮
9	既	既	既

石	一	丆	不
	石	石	
5			

只	丶	口	口
	只	只	
5			

隹	㇒	亻	亻	青	一	二	圭
	亻	亻	佳		主	圭	青
10	佳	隹	隻	8	青	青	
雞	㇒	⺈	幺	相	一	十	才
	幺	奚	鷄		木	朴	朴
18	雞	雞	雞	9	栩	相	相
蛋	㇖	㇕	下	鬥	丨	⺊	𠂆
	疋	疋	呑		𡰪	𡲆	鬥
11	呑	蛋	蛋	15	鬥	鬧	鬧
肉	丨	冂	内	重	㇒	二	亡
	内	肉	肉		亩	亩	盲
6				9	盲	重	重
趣	十	土	丰	主	丶	亠	亠
	走	走	赴		主	主	
15	趑	趙	趣	5			

普	゛	ソ	゛	忽	ノ	ク	ク
	並	並	並		勿	勿	忽
12	普	普	普	8	忽	忽	
通	⁻	⁻	⁻	推	一	扌	扌
	甬	甬	甬		扌	打	扩
11	通	通	通	11	拝	推	推
力	フ	力		惜	丶	丷	忄
					忄	忄	忄
2				11	惜	惜	惜
拉	一	扌	扌	誠	丶	一	言
	扌	扩	扩		言	訂	訪
8	拉	拉		13	誠	誠	誠
尺	フ	コ	尸	懶	忄	忄	忄
	尺				忄	悚	懶
4				19	懶	懶	懶

計	丶	亠	二	加	フ	カ	カ
	三	言	言		加	加	
9	言	計	計	5			
劃	マ	ヨ	聿	熟	二	古	亨
	聿	書	書		亨	亨	享
14	畫	劃	劃	15	孰	孰	熟
組	ㄥ	幺	幺	市	丶	亠	宀
	糹	糿	紉		市	市	
11	紀	組	組	5			
織	糹	紅	紒	縣	冂	月	目
	紅	締	繒		且	早	県
18	織	織	織	16	県	縣	縣
團	冂	冂	同	口	丶	冂	口
	圃	圍	團				
14	團	團	團	3			

產	亠	文	文	倍	亻	亻	亻
	产	产	产		亻	亻	位
11	產	產	產	10	倍	倍	倍
葉	艹	艹	艹	各	丿	勹	夂
	艹	苹	苹		夂	各	各
13	苹	葉	葉	6			
鐵	金	釒	釒	注	丶	冫	氵
	釒	釒	釒		氵	汁	汁
21	鐘	鐵	鐵	8	注	注	
解	丿	勹	角	政	一	丁	下
	角	角	角		正	正	正
13	解	解	解	9	政	政	政
或	一	一	口	府	丶	亠	广
	口	豆	或		广	庁	庐
8	或	或		8	府	府	

無	ノ	片	仁	向	ノ	亻	冂
	午	知	無		向	向	向
12	無	無	無	6			
線	幺	糸	糸	俗	ノ	亻	亻
	紀	紵	綧		亻	似	伙
15	線	線	線	9	伙	俗	俗
切	一	七	切	慣	忄	忄	忄
	切				忄	忄	忄
4				14	慣	慣	慣
裝	㇄	㇄	爿	言	丶	二	二
	牡	牡	牪		言	言	言
13	裝	裝	裝	7	言		
化	ノ	亻	亻	將	㇄	丬	爿
	化				將	將	將
4				11	將	將	將

濟	シ	汁	汸	迎	ノ	㇄	幻
	浐	济	浺		印	迎	迎
17	浺	濟	濟	8	迎	迎	
香	ノ	二	千	類	丷	米	半
	禾	禾	禾		类	类	类
9	香	香	香	19	類	類	類
器	口	吅	吅	論	丶	言	言
	哭	哭	哭		訁	訡	診
16	哭	器	器	15	論	論	論
油	丶	冫	シ	全	ノ	入	合
	汋	汭	汩		仐	全	全
8	油	油		6			
輕	一	日	亘	較	一	厂	币
	車	軒	輕		日	亘	車
14	輕	輕	輕	13	軒	軒	較

消	丶	丷	氵	部	丷	亠	立
	汁	沪	沪		产	音	音
10	沪	消	消	11	咅	部	部
架	フ	カ	カ	據	扌	护	抭
	加	加	加		捛	捛	據
9	架	架	架	16	據	據	據
蘇	艹	艿	苎	軍	丶	冖	冖
	茁	苗	蕒		冖	冃	冐
20	蘇	蘚	蘇	9	富	宣	軍
聯	丆	耳	耳	助	丨	冂	月
	耴	聫	聦		目	且	助
17	聮	聯	聯	7	助		
洋	丶	丷	氵	救	一	十	才
	沪	沪	沪		求	求	求
9	沪	洋	洋	11	救	救	救

員	丶	冂	口
	尸	吊	骨
10	骨	員	員

陸	㇇	阝	阝一
	阝十	阝坴	陸
11	陸	陸	陸

目	丨	冂	月
	目	目	
5			

危	丿	厃	危
	户	序	危
6			

基	一	廿	甘
	其	其	其
11	其	基	基

民	㇇	冖	尸
	民	民	
5			

雜	亠	六	卒
	亦	杂	剎
18	雜	雜	雜

降	㇇	阝	阝一
	阝㐄	阝夅	降
11	陊	降	降

誌	丶	言	言
	言	計	計
14	誌	誌	誌

落	十	卄	艾
	莎	莎	茨
13	落	落	落

COMPARATIVE TRANSCRIPTION TABLE

Yale   Wade-Giles   Pinyin

Yale	Wade-Giles	Pinyin	Yale	Wade-Giles	Pinyin
a	a	a	chye	ch'ieh	qie
ai	ai	ai	chyou	ch'iu	qiu
an	an	an	chyu	ch'ü	qu
ang	ang	ang	chyun	ch'ün	qun
au	ao	ao	chyung	ch'iung	qiong
			chywan	ch'üan	quan
ba	pa	ba	chywe	ch'üeh	que
bai	pai	bai			
ban	pan	ban	da	ta	da
bang	pang	bang	dai	tai	dai
bau	pao	bao	dan	tan	dan
bei	pei	bei	dang	tang	dang
ben	pen	ben	dau	tao	dao
beng	peng	beng	de	te	de
bi	pi	bi	dei	tei	dei
bin	pin	bin	deng	teng	deng
bing	ping	bing	di	ti	di
bou	pou	bou	ding	ting	ding
bu	pu	bu	dou	tou	dou
bwo	po	bo	du	tu	du
byan	pien	bian	dung	tung	dong
byau	piao	biao	dwan	tuan	duan
bye	pieh	bie	dwei	tui	dui
			dwo	to	duo
cha	ch'a	cha	dwun	tun	dun
chai	ch'ai	chai	dyan	tien	dian
chan	ch'an	chan	dyau	tiao	diao
chang	ch'ang	chang	dye	tieh	die
chau	ch'ao	chao	dyou	tiu	diu
che	ch'e	che	dz	tzu	zi
chen	ch'en	chen	dza	tsa	za
cheng	ch'eng	cheng	dzai	tsai	zai
chi	ch'i	qi	dzan	tsan	zan
chin	ch'in	qin	dzang	tsang	zang
ching	ch'ing	qing	dzau	tsao	zao
chou	ch'ou	chou	dze	tse	ze
chr	ch'ih	chi	dzei	tsei	zei
chu	ch'u	chu	dzen	tsen	zen
chung	ch'ung	chong	dzeng	tseng	zeng
chwai	ch'uai	chuai	dzou	tsou	zou
chwan	ch'uan	chuan	dzu	tsu	zu
chwang	ch'uang	chuang	dzung	tsung	zong
chwei	ch'ui	chui	dzwan	tsuan	zuan
chwo	ch'o	chuo	dzwei	tsui	zui
chwun	ch'un	chun	dzwo	tso	zuo
chya	ch'ia	qia	dzwun	tsun	zun
chyan	ch'ien	qian			
chyang	ch'iang	qiang	e	e, o	e
chyau	ch'iao	qiao	ei	ei	ei

Yale	Wade-Giles	Pinyin	Yale	Wade-Giles	Pinyin
en	en	en	jau	chao	zhao
eng	eng	eng	je	che	zhe
er	erh	er	jei	chei	zhei
			jen	chen	zhen
fa	fa	fa	jeng	cheng	zheng
fan	fan	fan	ji	chi	ji
fang	fang	fang	jin	chin	jin
fei	fei	fei	jing	ching	jing
fen	fen	fen	jou	chou	zhou
feng	feng	feng	jr	chih	'zhi
fou	fou	fou	ju	chu	zhu
fu	fu	fu	jung	chung	zhong
fwo	fo	fo	jwa	chua	zhua
			jwai	chuai	zhuai
ga	ka	ga	jwan	chuan	zhuan
gai	kai	gai	jwang	chuang	zhuang
gan	kan	gan	jwei	chui	zhui
gang	kang	gang	jwo	cho	zhuo
gau	kao	gao	jwun	chun	zhun
ge	ke, ko	ge	jya	chia	jia
gei	kei	gei	jyan	chien	jian
gen	ken	gen	jyang	chiang	jiang
geng	keng	geng	jyau	chiao	jiao
gou	kou	gou	jye	chieh	jie
gu	ku	gu	jyou	chiu	jiu
gung	kung	gong	jyu	chü	ju
gwa	kua	gua	jyun	chün	jun
gwai	kuai	guai	jyung	chiung	jiong
gwan	kuan	guan	jywan	chüan	juan
gwang	kuang	guang	jywe	chüeh	jue
gwei	kuei	gui			
gwo	kuo	guo	ka	k'a	ka
gwun	kun	gun	kai	k'ai	kai
			kan	k'an	kan
ha	ha	ha	kang	k'ang	kang
hai	hai	hai	kau	k'ao	kao
han	han	han	ke	k'e, k'o	ke
hang	hang	hang	ken	k'en	ken
hau	hao	hao	keng	k'eng	keng
he	ho	he	kou	k'ou	kou
hei	hei	hei	ku	k'u	ku
hen	hen	hen	kung	k'ung	kong
heng	heng	heng	kwa	k'ua	kua
hou	hou	hou	kwai	k'uai	kuai
hu	hu	hu	kwan	k'uan	kuan
hung	hung	hong	kwang	k'uang	kuang
hwa	hua	hua	kwei	k'uei	kui
hwai	huai	huai	kwo	k'uo	kuo
hwan	huan	huan	kwun	k'un	kun
hwang	huang	huang			
hwei	hui	hui	la	la	la
hwo	huo	huo	lai	lai	lai
hwun	hun	hun	lan	lan	lan
			lang	lang	lang
ja	cha	zha	lau	lao	lao
jai	chai	zhai	le	le	le
jan	chan	zhan	lei	lei	lei
jang	chang	zhang	leng	leng	leng

Yale	Wade-Giles	Pinyin	Yale	Wade-Giles	Pinyin
li	li	li	nyau	niao	niao
lin	lin	lin	nye	nieh	nie
ling	ling	ling	nyou	niu	niu
lou	lou	lou	nyu	nü	nü
lu	lu	lu	nywe	nüeh	nüe
lung	lung	long			
lwan	luan	luan	ou	ou	ou
lwo	lo	luo			
lwun	lun	lun	pa	p'a	pa
lya	lia	lia	pai	p'ai	pai
lyan	lien	lian	pan	p'an	pan
lyang	liang	liang	pang	p'ang	pang
lyau	liao	liao	pau	p'ao	pao
lye	lieh	lie	pei	p'ei	pei
lyou	liu	liu	pen	p'en	pen
lyu	lü	lü	peng	p'eng	peng
lywan	lüan	lüan	pi	p'i	pi
lywe	lüeh	lüe	pin	p'in	pin
			ping	p'ing	ping
ma	ma	ma	pou	p'ou	pou
mai	mai	mai	pu	p'u	pu
man	man	man	pwo	p'o	po
mang	mang	mang	pyan	p'ien	pian
mau	mao	mao	pyau	p'iao	piao
mei	mei	mei	pye	p'ieh	pie
men	men	men			
meng	meng	meng	r	jih	ri
mi	mi	mi	ran	jan	ran
min	min	min	rang	jang	rang
ming	ming	ming	rau	jao	rao
mou	mou	mou	re	je	re
mu	mu	mu	ren	jen	ren
mwo	mo	mo	reng	jeng	reng
myan	mien	mian	rou	jou	rou
myau	miao	miao	ru	ju	ru
mye	mieh	mie	rung	jung	rong
myou	miu	miu	rwan	juan	ruan
			rwei	jui	rui
na	na	na	rwo	jo	ruo
nai	nai	nai	rwun	jun	run
nan	nan	nan			
nang	nang	nang	sa	sa	sa
nau	nao	nao	sai	sai	sai
ne	ne	ne	san	san	san
nei	nei	nei	sang	sang	sang
nen	nen	nen	sau	sao	sao
neng	neng	neng	se	se	se
ni	ni	ni	sen	sen	sen
nin	nin	nin	seng	seng	seng
ning	ning	ning	sha	sha	sha
nou	nou	nou	shai	shai	shai
nu	nu	nu	shan	shan	shan
nung	nung	nong	shang	shang	shang
nwan	nuan	nuan	shau	shao	shao
nwo	no	nuo	she	she	she
nwun	nun	nun	shei	shei	shei
nyan	nien	nian	shen	shen	shen
nyang	niang	niang	sheng	sheng	sheng

Yale	Wade-Giles	Pinyin	Yale	Wade-Giles	Pinyin
shou	shou	shou	tsau	ts'ao	cao
shr	shih	shi	tse	ts'e	ce
shu	shu	shu	tsen	ts'en	cen
shwa	shua	shua	tseng	ts'eng	ceng
shwai	shuai	shuai	tsou	ts'ou	cou
shwan	shuan	shuan	tsu	ts'u	cu
shwang	shuang	shuang	tsung	ts'ung	cong
shwei	shui	shui	tswan	ts'uan	cuan
shwo	shuo	shuo	tswei	ts'ui	cui
shwun	shun	shun	tswo	ts'o	cuo
sou	sou	sou	tswun	ts'un	cun
su	su	su	tsz	tz'u	ci
sung	sung	song	tu	t'u	tu
swan	suan	suan	tung	t'ung	tong
swei	sui	sui	twan	t'uan	tuan
swo	so	suo	twei	t'ui	tui
swun	sun	sun	two	t'o	tuo
sya	hsia	xia	twun	t'un	tun
syan	hsien	xian	tyan	t'ien	tian
syang	hsiang	xiang	tyau	t'iao	tiao
syau	hsiao	xiao	tye	t'ieh	tie
sye	hsieh	xie			
syi	hsi	xi	wa	wa	wa
syin	hsin	xin	wai	wai	wai
sying	hsing	xing	wan	wan	wan
syou	hsiu	xiu	wang	wang	wang
syu	hsü	xu	wei	wei	wei
syun	hsün	xun	wen	wen	wen
syung	hsiung	xiong	weng	weng	weng
sywan	hsüan	xuan	wo	wo	wo
sywe	hsüeh	xue	wu	wu	wu
sz	ssu, szu	si			
			ya	ya	ya
ta	t'a	ta	yai	yai	yai
tai	t'ai	tai	yan	yen	yan
tan	t'an	tan	yang	yang	yang
tang	t'ang	tang	yau	yao	yao
tau	t'ao	tao	ye	yeh	ye
te	t'e	te	yi	yi, i	yi
teng	t'eng	teng	yin	yin	yin
ti	t'i	ti	ying	ying	ying
ting	t'ing	ting	you	yu	you
tou	t'ou	tou	yu	yü	yu
tsa	ts'a	ca	yun	yün	yun
tsai	ts'ai	cai	yung	yung	yong
tsan	ts'an	can	ywan	yüan	yuan
tsang	ts'ang	cang	ywe	yüeh	yue

The following pages present lesson by lesson the Sentences (jyudz/juzi) section of each lesson printed in simplified characters.

第一课　句　子

1. 今年夏天你打算到海边儿去吗？我有两个姐姐都
　　打算去。

2. 要是你想去我可以给你们介绍 ²²介绍。

3. 我二姐是北海大学的学生，今年冬天就要毕业了。

4. 我刚才 ²³接着 ²⁴他的信，那封信上说他明天就可以到
　　上海了。

5. 他打算在家里住三四个月，再 ²⁵回北京去。

6. 他这次回北京去大概要等毕业以后才回家。

7. 我家住在乡下离城大概三十里路。

8. 要是你想到我家去你最好预先告诉我，我可以到
　　车站去接你。

9. 我们乡下有一个很好的旅馆 ²⁶，我可以给你预定 ²⁷一
　　个屋子。

10. 听说你今年秋天要到北京去念书，我想你最好跟
　　我二姐谈谈。

11. 他在北京有很多朋友，我想他一定可以给你介绍
　　几个。

12. 你刚才说的那位王先生，他也是北海大学毕业的
　　吗？我二姐大概认识他。

13. 我大姐现在在美国念书，他大概今年夏天可以回国。

14. 我一共有两个姐姐，大姐姐在美国，二姐姐在北京。

15. 我刚才说的是我大姐，不是我二姐。

16. 我刚才接着大姐的信，信上说在美国念书真有意思。

17. 听说他的学校离海边儿不远。

18. 我不知道有多少里，我想大概有二三十里吧。

19. 我大姐每个礼拜给我写一封信，上个月我一共接着他四封信。

20. 今年春天我接着他的一封信，信上说他今年夏天就可以毕业了。

21. 毕业以后他想到别的地方去玩儿。

22. 他说美国的乡下很有意思，他毕业以后一定要到乡下去住一个月。

23. 听说这次毕业一共有五个中国学生，他们今年冬天回国。

24. 我已经给大姐写了一封信，要他毕了业就回来。

25. 要是你要知道一点儿美国大学的事情，你可以跟

我大姐谈谈。

26．你不认识他，不要紧，我可以给你们介绍。

27．我大姐很喜欢谈话，他常跟他的朋友谈一天的话。

28．他常常预备 ²⁸了很多点心，请很多朋友到他家去吃
点心。

29．我大姐说，他的外国朋友都喜欢吃他预备的中国
点心。

30．你想给我大姐写信吗？我这儿有信纸信封 ²⁹。

第二课　句　子

1. 上礼拜我接到李先生的一封航空信，信上说，他
　　跟他姐姐要到这儿来旅行 [18]。

2. 他问我这儿的风景好不好。夏天热不热。

3. 他还问我这儿的旅馆 [19] 干净不干净。

4. 要是旅馆干净，他要我替他预定一间房间。

5. 我很想见见李先生，特别想见他姐姐，所以我想
　　给他们打一个电话。

6. 可是打电话恐怕很贵，所以我想最好到电报局去
　　给他们打一个电报。

7. 可是我有很多话要跟李先生说，打电报恐怕也很
　　贵，所以我给他们寄了一封航空信。

8. 我告诉他们说，这儿是一个乡下地方，春天跟秋
　　天时候的风景特别好。

9. 夏天不太热，可是冬天的天气很干，风也很大。

10. 这儿的旅馆很多，也很干净，可是很贵。

11. 我家有很多空 [20] 屋子，我可以给你们收拾两间，你
　　们就不用住旅馆了。

12. 过了几天我又收到李先生的一封航空信。

13. 信上说，他因为有要紧的事情，恐怕不能来旅行，

所以他要他姐姐一个人来。

14. 他谢谢我这么热心。他要我到火车站接他姐姐去。

15. 李小姐 [21] 一下火车就问我，我的车在哪儿，他说他的行李很多。

16. 我说我没有车，我们得坐电车 [22] 回去，他听了很生气。

17. 他说他有很多行李，恐怕不能坐电车。我说不要紧，我可以替他拿。

18. 他问我邮局 [23] 在哪儿，他要去寄一封信，告诉他的弟弟他已经很平安的到了。

19. 我说火车站后头的那间小屋子就是邮局。

20. 李小姐说，我们这儿的邮局又小又不干净。

21. 我们到了家，我替他把行李放在一间收拾好了的屋子里。

22. 他看了看那间屋子说：「这间屋子太小，我想我到旅馆去住吧。」

23. 我说这儿的旅馆都很贵。他说贵不要紧，可是得干净。

24. 我带他到风景好的地方去看看，他说这儿的风景没有什么特别。

25. 我问他打算在这儿住几天，他说他打算明天早上
    就回去。

26. 我预备了晚饭，可是他说他得收拾行李，没有工
    夫到我家来吃晚饭。

27. 第二天早上我替他把行李送到火车站去。

28. 他要我替他打一个电报，叫他弟弟到火车站去接
    他。

29. 我送他上火车，跟他说一路平安，请他有工夫再
    到这儿来玩儿。

30. 他说他不太喜欢旅行，所以恐怕不会再来了。

第三课 句 子

1. 请问到<u>上海</u>去的飞机什么时候起飞[23]？

2. 对不起，我的国语不好，说不清楚，我刚才说的是到<u>上海</u>去的飞机。

3. 下午四点零五分才起飞吗？为什么上午没有飞机起飞呢？

4. 我得立刻到票房去买票。票房的门还没开吗？我们坐下谈谈吧。

5. 先生，你也坐今天下午的飞机到<u>上海</u>去吗？

6. 你要坐飞机到<u>北京</u>去吗？我以为你也要到<u>上海</u>去。

7. <u>北京</u>离这儿就有一百里路，你为什么不坐汽车去呢？

8. 听说北京那个地方非常有意思，我希望我有机会[24]到那儿去旅行。

9. 我小的时候跟我姐姐去过一次，可是现在都不记得了。

10. 那一次是坐汽车去的，我记得我坐了一天的汽车。

11. 我记不清楚我那个时候住在什么地方了，大概住在离城不远的一个乡下。

12 · 我记得我们每天早上坐汽车到城里去，中午就在
　　邮局前头的那个饭馆儿吃饭。

13 · 我记得北京的风景非常好，地方也很干净，可是
　　夏天很热。

14 · 现在才三点零七分，别着急 ²⁵，我们还可以谈一会
　　儿。

15 · 你的国语说得这么好，你一定是北京人吧？

16 · 你是在北海大学毕业的吗？我姐姐也是在北海大
　　学毕业的。

17 · 我不记得他是哪年毕的业。让我想一想，对了，
　　大概是一九六〇年吧。

18 · 他的国语说得非常好，简直的跟北京人说得一样。

19 · 我希望我的国语说得跟他一样好。

20 · 要是我有机会到北京去，我一定到你家去看你。

21 · 到上海去的飞机已经来了吗？在这儿停几分钟？

22 · 就停十分钟吗？我还没买票呢！我得立刻就走。

23 · 我不着急。这是我第一次坐飞机。我的皮包在哪
　　儿呢？

24 · 我知道带飞机不能带太多行李，所以我一共就带
　　两个小皮包。

25. 这个皮包是我自己的，那个皮包是我姐姐让我替
    他带去的。
26. 我不知道从这儿到<u>上海</u>得几个钟头。要是哪儿都
    不停大概半天就可以到了。
27. 你的飞机什么时候起飞？你怎么一点儿也不着急
    呢？
28. 你已经买飞机票了吗？我以为你还没买呢。
29. 票房的门大概已经开了，我真立刻得走了。
30. 希望有机会再跟你谈谈，再见，一路平安。

第四课　句　子

1．我去年春天到<u>德国</u>去旅行的时候，我到一个鞋铺去买鞋。

2．铺子里的人问我穿几号的鞋。喜欢什么颜色。

3．我告诉他我要买一双深黄的皮鞋，可是我不记得穿几号的鞋。

4．因为我的<u>德国</u>话说得不太好，所以他没听清楚。

5．他给了我一双深红的皮鞋。我说：「不成，不成。」

6．他给我换了一双浅红的布鞋，我还说：「不成，不成。」

7．我说，我要深黄的皮鞋，不要浅红的布鞋。

8．后来他听清楚了。他给我换了一双深黄的皮鞋，要我试一试。

9．我试了试，觉得不合适。　我问他那双鞋几号。他说六号。

10．我说六号的不合适，请你给我换一双七号的吧。

11．他给我换了一双七号的，可是我还觉得不合适。

12. 后来他量 [25] 了量我的脚，他说，我应当穿六号半
    的鞋。

13. 我试了试六号半的，觉得很合适。我说：「成，六
    号半的很合适。」

14. 可是我不喜欢这个鞋的样子。他说这是最新式的
    皮鞋。

15. 我问他价钱贵不贵。他说：「价钱不贵，价钱不贵。」

16. 我回国以后，我的朋友都说，我鞋的样子好。

17. 很多人跟我商量，要我替他们买鞋。

18. 我说我有一个朋友姓李，他是一个德国的商人 [27]，
    我可以跟他商量，请他替你们买。

19. 我给李先生写了一封航空信，请他替我的朋友买
    鞋。

20. 李先生说：「成，可是你得告诉我那个鞋铺在哪儿。」

21. 我又给他写了一封航空信说：「鞋铺在邮局的前头，
    楼上是旅馆，楼下是鞋铺。」

22. 他问我：「一共要几双？什么颜色？几号？」

23. 我说：「一共要买两双，一双皮鞋，一
    双布鞋。

24. 皮鞋请买七号，深红的；布鞋请买六号，浅黄的。」

25. 那年的秋天我接着李先生的一封信，信上说：「鞋
    已经寄走了 [28]，请你们收到 [29]以后立刻试一试，要
    是不合适可以寄回来换。」

26. 我们收到鞋以后大家都试了，都觉得很合适。

27. 大家都说德国鞋真不错，样子好，价钱也不贵。

28. 后来又有很多朋友要我给他们介绍李先生。

29. 我说：「不成，买鞋的人太多了，李先生恐怕不愿
    意帮忙。

30. 我给你们介绍那个鞋铺，你们自己给那个鞋铺写
    信吧。」

第五课　句　子

1. 谢谢你，我不抽烟。你刚才说你要租房吗？我现在住的那所²⁵房可以让你住。

2. 我今年冬天就要毕业了，毕业以后想到德国去留学²⁶。

3. 那所房在乡下，离这儿大概有十里路。

4. 前头是海，后头是山。房子虽然不大，可是风景很好。

5. 夏天一点儿不热，晚上，海上的风特别大。

6. 一共有四间屋子，楼上两间，楼下两间，房子里的东西很简单，可是很新。

7. 你结婚了没有？象这样的房子给结婚的人住，合适极了。

8. 你跟你太太离婚²⁷了吗？没有关系，那位房东也离过一次婚。

9. 屋里当然可以抽烟。孩子说话的声音大也没有关系。

10. 房租按月算。按礼拜算都可以。要是按月算，每月六十块钱。

11. 不管灯，水。灯，水每月大概十块钱。

12. 你打算在这儿住多久 [28]，要是住得很久，房租也许
    可以少一点儿。

13. 你跟房东谈一谈。你需要 [29] 什么可以告诉他。

14. 要是你开汽车去半个钟头就到了。房子的墙 [30] 是红
    颜色的，很容易找。

15. 你暂时不能决定吗？没有关系，你不管什么时候
    决定都成。

16. 你可以先留一点儿定钱，请他给你留一个礼拜。

17. 报上的房子出租广告虽然很多，可是象那样合适
    的房子很少。

18. 我租那所房子的时候，是看见了广告才找着的。

19. 我看见的不是报上的广告，是墙上的广告。

20. 那天我在乡下玩儿，看见墙上有一张房子出租的
    广告。

21. 按那个地方的人说，那所房子已经很久没租出去
    了。

22. 我见了房东，房东说，那所房子暂时不能住，因
    为水管子 [31] 跟电灯 [32] 都还没收拾好。

23. 我说，我已经决定租那所房子了，不管 [33] 有没有灯，

水我都得租。

24． 我立刻留了二十块钱的定钱。虽然房东说不需要
　　留定钱，可是我还是留了。

25． 房东说：「这个房子里的东西很简单，你需要什么
　　东西可以跟我说。」

26． 我说：「我暂时不需要什么，要是以后我需要什么，
　　我一定告诉你。」

27． 我在那儿住了很久。我希望这次到德国去留学能
　　找到象这样的房子。

28． 我决定十一月一号上午坐十点零五分的飞机到德
　　国去。

29． 我走以前你们可以暂时住几个月的旅馆。

30． 那位房东虽然是上海人，可是国语说得很好。你
　　跟他说话的时候声音得大一点儿。

第六课　句　子

1. 我得立刻到警察局去。我家昨天夜里来了一个贼，
　　偷了很多东西去。

2. 你为什么不给警察局打一个电话，请他们派一个
　　警察来呢？

3. 好，可是我记不清楚警察局的电话多少号了。

4. 那个贼偷了一些什么东西，那些东西都保险了没
　　有？

5. 那个贼偷了我一个金表，一个皮包，一双浅
　　黄颜色的皮鞋，还有很多银的东西。

6. 你不应该把金的跟银的东西放在家里，你为什么
　　不放在银行里呢？

7. 本来是放在银行里的，昨天才取出来，我以为警
　　察局离我家不到 ²³一公里 ²⁴路，一定没有贼敢 ²⁵来偷
　　东西。

8. 除了那些金的，银的东西以外还偷了别的东西没
　　有？

9. 还有一些铜的东西，不值什么钱，最值钱的是那
　　个金表。

10. 是一个什么样的金表？值多少钱？

11．那个表是我姐姐的，是一个德国表，五年以前值
　　两百块美金，现在的价钱当然比以前贵多了。

12．我刚才给我姐姐写了一封航空信，可是还没寄呢。

13．我回去的时候我的汽车可以在邮局停一停，替你
　　去寄那封航空信。

14．你那些东西都保险了吧？你给保险公司 ²⁶打电话了
　　吗 ²⁷？

15．我刚才给保险公司打电话了，他们要我把偷了的
　　东西开一张单子 ²⁸，等一会儿他们就派人来。

16．你应该开两张单子，一张给保险公司，一张给警
　　察局。

17．单子已经开好了，可是有很多东西的价钱我记不
　　清楚了。

18．那个贼进来的时候你已经睡着了吗？

19．那个贼大概是夜里十一点钟进来的。那个时候我
　　还没睡着。

20．我看见一个穿深黄衣裳的人从窗户那儿
　　进来。

21．你看见那个贼进来，为什么不大声叫呢？

22．因为我看见那个贼比我高，也比我结实，所以我

没敢叫。

23. 那个贼非常客气的警告 [29] 我说：「我来取一点儿东西，
　　请不要怕，也不要大声叫。」

24. 我说，这儿实在没有什么值钱的东西，桌子上的
　　那些东西都是铜作的。」

25. 他说，「没有关系，铜作的东西很结实，比金子作
　　的好。」

26. 他看了看我姐姐的那个德国表说：「这个表很值钱
　　吧？」

27. 我说：「这是一个旧式 [30] 的表，不值什么钱，你拿另
　　外那个银的吧。」

28. 他说：「除了这个金表以外，你还有一个银的吗？
　　好极了，我都要。」

29. 他走的时候说：「我取的东西你都记清楚了吗？明
　　天你可以告诉保险公司，跟公司要钱。」

30. 他走了以后我不敢起来，也不敢给警察局打电话。
　　我恐怕他还在门外头等着我呢。

第七课　句　子

1. 我很久没看见王先生了。有的人说他已经死了，
   有的人说他还活着呢。

2. 我第一次看见王先生是在一个教堂里。一个朋友
   给我们介绍的。

3. 我觉得他是世界上最奇怪的人，可是他对地理 ³²很
   有研究 ³³。

4. 不管是春天或是夏天，他老穿一件旧的布衣
   裳，从来没换过。

5. 他住的那间屋子又小又不干净，浅红颜色的墙已
   经成了黑颜色的了。

6. 桌上有很多书，那些书多半儿是地理书。

7. 他的生活 ³⁴苦极了，可是他说，他一点儿也不苦。

8. 我先以为他很穷，后来我知道他不穷。

9. 有一次我有要紧的事情，得坐飞机到上海去。我
   需要一百块钱买飞机票。

10. 可是那天是星期六，银行不开门，所以我取不着
    钱。

11. 王先生说：「我这儿有钱，你拿去用吧，反正我暂

时不需要。」

12. 他不高兴的时候就低着头不理 [35] 人。

13. 他高兴的时候就给人讲很多故事。

14. 他讲的故事都很有道理。 有的时候道理太深了我
    就不懂了。

15. 有的时候他低着头，很静的，半天不说话，好象 [36]
    睡着了一样。

16. 有的时候我想约 [37] 他到街上去玩儿。他说街上的人
    太多，不安静。

17. 有的时候我想约他到上海去旅行。 他说火车票太
    贵，他很穷，买不起票。

18. 可是我每次约他到教堂去作礼拜，他都不反对 [38]，
    很高兴的跟我去。

19. 有一次我问他结婚了没有。 他说结婚了，可是太
    太死了。

20. 我又问他为什么不再结婚。 他低着头，半天没说
    话。

21. 后来他说，在这个世界上不容易找着一位合适的
    小姐。

22. 我说我可以给他介绍一位合适的小姐。他笑着说，

谁愿意跟一个象他那么穷的人结婚呢。

23．有一个星期日我到教堂去作礼拜，可是那天<u>王</u>先生没去。

24．我到他家去找他，他没在家。按房东说，他已经三天没回家了。

25．春天过去 ^{39} 了，夏天也过去了，可是我一直没再看见过<u>王</u>先生。有的人说他已经死了，有的人说他还活着呢。

26．有一天我在<u>上海</u>乡下的一个教堂里作礼拜。那天作礼拜的人很多，教堂里快坐满了。

27．我看见一个人很象<u>王</u>先生。我高兴极了，想立刻走过去 ^{40} 叫他。

28．可是教堂里很安静，我不能大声的叫。

29．那个人没理我，低着头，从另外一个门出去了。

30．我真希望有一天<u>王</u>先生会回来给我讲很多故事。

第八课　句　子

1. 老李的信上常说，他们的学校有很大的运动场跟图书馆。

2. 他说他不常到运动场去，因为他不太喜欢运动。

3. 可是他每天到图书馆去，因为在那儿念书很安静。

4. 图书馆的外头有树，有草地，所以夏天很凉快。

5. 他常常一个人在树下头休息，听鸟儿叫。

6. 有的时候他们在图书馆上课，因为图书馆比课堂[24]凉快。

7. 我很想去参观参观他们的学校，可是我不敢去，因为我不会说国语。

8. 他说，不会说国语没有关系，因为他们的学校里有很多从别省去的学生，他们的国语都说得不太好。

9. 他要我今年冬天，学校放假以后，去参观。因为学校规定，放假的时候学校可以让人参观。

10. 可是我听说，北方[25]的冬天很冷，常下雪，所以我不敢去。

11. 老李说，今年秋天学校里有一个运动会[26]，所以放三天假。

12. 我给老李写了一封航空信，告诉他，我决定坐十

　　月十二号下午一点零五分的特别快车到北京去。

13. 我请他替我租一间屋子，因为我想在那儿休息一

　　个星期。

14. 我到了北京，老李没到车站来接我，我非常着急。

15. 虽然是秋天，可是那天的天气很冷，外头下着雪。

16. 我跟站上的人说：「我是刚从别省来的。请问，哪

　　儿有旅馆？」

17. 他说：「往东走，过一条街²⁷，有很多大树，树后头

　　有一个草绿颜色的楼，那就是旅馆。」

18. 他说：「外头下着雪呢，冷极了，你在这儿休息一

　　会儿吧。」

19. 我给老李的学校打了一个电话。学校里的人说，

　　老李上着课呢。他们学校规定，上课的时候学

　　生不可以接电话²⁸。

20. 我在街上走了半天，可是没看见草绿颜色的楼，

　　也没看见什么大树。

21. 那个时候雪下得大极了。我觉得很冷，所以我在

　　一个铺子里买了一包²⁹烟，喝了一点儿热茶。我

　　又买了一张北京地图³⁰。

22. 我打算立刻坐火车回南方 ³¹去，可是那个时候老李
　　来了。

23. 他说，他没收到我的信。我说，大概是邮局送错
　　了。

24. 我在北京一共住了三天。每天都下雪，每天都很
　　冷。我实在不喜欢那种天气。

25. 老李要我明年夏天再到北京去，因为明年夏天他
　　要毕业了。

26. 他说，夏天北京的风景好极了，哪儿都有树，有
　　绿的草地，哪儿都有鸟儿叫。

27. 他要我在上海替他买一双最新式的，草绿颜
　　色的德国皮鞋。

28. 他说：「这种皮鞋北京买不着。你买了以后请立刻
　　寄给我。价钱贵，不要紧。」

29. 我在上海没买着草绿颜色的皮鞋，所以我给他寄
　　了一双浅黄颜色的。

30. 他来信说，我买的那双皮鞋，大小很合适，
　　可是他不喜欢那种颜色。

第九课　句　子

1. 我还记得老高，他上历史课的时候总坐在我的左边儿。

2. 他常常举手问问题，有的时候他的问题很奇怪，连先生都不能回答。

3. 要是先生问我们一个问题，他总是第一个举手，虽然他不一定会回答。

4. 他也学俄文，他说，学俄文得常练习。

5. 有的时候他用俄文问我一个问题，我没用俄文回答，他就不高兴。

6. 他常常借我的历史书去看。他说，他很穷，买不起书。

7. 他说，他父母活着的时候很有钱，家里有很多金的跟银的东西。

8. 可是他十岁的时候父母都死了，所以他越来越穷了。

9. 有一个冬天的夜里，他家来了一个贼，把值钱的东西都偷走了。

10. 警察局虽然派了很多警察去找那个贼，可是没找

着。

11. 后来他苦极了，苦得连饭都吃不起。

12. 现在他白天在一个公司里卖布，晚上到学校里来
　　　念书。

13. 我问他结婚了没有。他说，他连饭都吃不起，哪
　　　儿有钱结婚。

14. 有一天老高到我家来，对我说，他需要六十块钱。
　　　他问我能不能暂时借给他。

15. 他说他没有钱给房租。房东太太很利害。要是他
　　　不给钱就不能在那儿住。

16. 我说我得到银行去取。我约他明天到我家来取钱。

17. 第二天老高来了。我交给²⁹他七十块钱。我说：「另
　　　外的十块钱给你买皮鞋。你的那双皮鞋应
　　　该换了。」

18. 老高说：「皮鞋太贵，我去买一双布鞋吧。反
　　　正布鞋也很结实，何必非买皮鞋不可呢！」

19. 春假³⁰的时候我想约老高到乡下去休息几天。他说：
　　　「旅行又费钱³¹又费时候，我不去。」

20. 我在乡下病了，病得很利害。我真希望有朋友来
　　　看看我。

21. 老高听说我病了，就来看我。他是坐飞机来的。

22. 我问他，买飞机票的钱是谁给他的。他说他是跟
     他的公司借的。

23. 春假以后我很久没看见老高。上历史课的时候他
     也没去。

24. 有一天晚上我到他家去。他屋子里的灯没开。我
     想他一定没在家。我在屋子外头等了一会儿就
     走了。

25. 我回家的时候看见墙上有一封信。

26. 我一看就知道是老高写的。他说他没有钱，所以
     不能再念书了。

27. 他说，这个世界上不念书的人反正也可以生活，
     何必非念书不可。

28. 他说，他有一个朋友介绍他到广东省去作事。他
     已经决定走了。

29. 老高走了。我们上历史课的时候没有人再举手问
     问题。

30. 有一天我刚考完社会学，我收到老高的一封很简
     单的信。信上说，他那儿的情形很好。

第十课　句　子

1. 去年夏天，我常常头痛，发烧，不知道是什么原故。

2. 后来我到一个私立医院去查病[20]，那个医院离这儿就有三公里。

3. 医院里的人问我，是内科是外科。我说，我不知道。

4. 我告诉他，我头痛，发烧。那个人要我到二楼去。

5. 我在二楼等了半天。有一个护士跟我说，该我了[23]。

6. 那位医生姓李。李医生给我检查了半天，又给我试了试温度。

7. 医生说，我的温度不高，没什么病。他给了我一包药。

8. 我不知道是什么药，是深红的，有一点儿象红铜[24]的颜色。

9. 我要他给我照一张 X 光。他说，我不用照 X 光。

10. 他说，我吃了这包药就不头痛，不发烧了。

11. 我把那包药吃了，可是还觉得头痛，发烧。

12. 医生又试了试我的温度，问了我很多问题。

13. 他问我在哪儿作事？抽烟不抽烟？

14 · 我说，我在一个私立中学念书。平常一天大概抽
　　 一包烟，忙的时候一天抽一包半。

15 · 吃饭的时候，不管吃什么东西都觉得没有味儿。

16 · 医生要我暂时在医院留几天。他要给我好好儿
　　 的检查检查。

17 · 医院里的风景很好，有很多树。我最喜欢一个人
　　 坐在树底下听鸟儿叫。

18 · 可是那几天每天都下雨，所以我除了吃饭以外就
　　 给朋友写信。

19 · 我在医院住了三天，一共写了二十封航空信。

20 · 每天中午我请一位护士替我到邮局寄信去。

21 · 我随时 ²⁵ 都想回去，可是护士说，他们医院规定，
　　 病人 ²⁶不可以随便出去。

22 · 我跟护士说，我在一个私立中学念书。那个私立
　　 中学的功课 ²⁷特别忙。

23 · 后来医生来了，医生说，我的病是因为念书太用
　　 功的原故。

24 · 他说，这是一种新发现 ²⁸的病。现在科学家 ²⁹正在研
　　 究，还没有发明 ³⁰什么新药。

25 · 他要我回去以后常常到运动场去运动，随时出去

照照象 ³¹，玩儿玩儿。

26. 我说，我秋天就要毕业了，毕业以前我一定常常
    到学校的运动场去运动。

27. 医生说，要是我觉得头痛，发烧，可以随时去看
    他。

28. 我回家以后常常运动，没有事的时候就开着汽车
    出去玩儿。

29. 那年秋天的毕业考试，我考得不太好，可是我觉
    得很值得 ³²。

30. 因为我回家以后一直的没病过 ³³，不管吃什么东西
    都觉得味儿不错。

第十一课　句　子

1．一九六〇年的夏天，我母亲死了。那个时候我的
　　身体跟精神都非常坏。

2．有一天我的同学黄子安来看我。他一看见我就说：
　　「你的身体跟精神怎么这么坏呢！」

3．他说，他家在乡下，那儿的风景很好，有湖，有
　　树，有花儿；还有好看的石头。

4．他说：「你需要休息，要是你同意到我家去住，对
　　你的身体跟精神一定有好处。」

5．我原来不想去。我想在同学家住不如在自己家住。

6．而且我家的花园子 ²³ 不错。虽然没有湖，可是到处
　　都有花儿，到处都有石头，何必非到乡下去不可
　　呢。

7．可是子安很热心，一定要我去，所以我只好说：
　　「你既然一定要我去，我就去住一个星期吧。」

8．那是我第一次看见子安的姐姐，子英，那天他穿
　　了一件深绿颜色的布衣裳。

9．他的那双浅黄的皮鞋虽然样子不太新，可
　　是很合适。

10． 子安给我们介绍了以后，子英小姐就对我说：「我
　　　已经给您收拾了一间屋子，您要洗洗脸，
　　　换换衣裳吗？」

11． 我们不久就成²⁴了很好的朋友。他听说我是研究社
　　　会学的，所以常常问我社会学的问题。

12． 他的问题虽然很简单，可是我总觉得我回答得不
　　　够清楚。

13． 子英的国语虽然说得不太好，可是他会说德文也
　　　会说俄文，他常要跟我练习说德文。

14． 可是我的德文说得不如他，所以我只好说，我不
　　　会说。

15． 我们常一块儿在湖边儿上打球，坐在石头上谈话。

16． 有的时候我们谈历史，地理；有的时候我们也谈
　　　看电影跟听戏。

17． 乡下的天气好极了，差不多每天都有太阴，从来
　　　不下雨，并且也不太热。

18． 我在乡下住了三个月，差不多天天打球，我的身
　　　体比以前结实多了，作事情也有精神了。

19． 有一天我接着从广东省寄来的一封航空信，那封
　　　信是我从前的一个同事²⁵写的。

20. 他说，他在广东省有一个保险公司，希望我能去
    参观，而且希望我能帮他作一点儿事。

21. 我动身²⁶的那一天，子安跟子英送我到飞机场²⁷去。
    子英说再见的时候，声音很低，好象快哭了。

22. 我总觉得广东那个地方不如北京。那儿的花儿不
    如北京的好看；那儿的石头不如北京的奇怪；
    那儿的湖也不如北京的有意思。

23. 虽然我常去听戏，打球，可是我的精神越来越
    坏。我觉得在那儿作事对我没有好处；我觉得
    苦极了。

24. 可是我既然来了当然不能随便走，所以我跟那个
    同事商量，告诉他，我想回北京去。

25. 那个同事很同情我。他说：「没有关系，你回去吧。」

26. 一九六一年的冬天，我给黄家打了一个电报，告
    诉他们，我坐十二月四号早上八点零五分的飞
    机回北京。

27. 我下飞机的时侯就看见子安一个人来接我。他说，
    子英今年春天已经结婚了，而且快有孩子了。

28. 我既然到了北京，当然应该去看看子英，可是子
    安不同意。他说，子英这两天身体不好，最好

不去看他。

29. 我在<u>黄</u>家住了两天。我觉得湖边儿上不如以前好
    玩儿；石头也不如以前好看；连太阴都不如以
    前。

30. 我觉得世界上什么东西都没有意思；我也不知道
    为什么我还活在这个没有意思的世界上。

第十二课　句　子

1. 我还记得我年青的时候，在一个私立大学念书的情形。

2. 老何，小张跟我三个人住在一块儿，很热闹。

3. 老何有六尺多高，比普通人高半尺。小张只有五尺高。他们两个人都很诚实。

4. 我们的房子在乡下，房租按月算，每月六十块钱，管灯，水。

5. 我们那儿离学校有十里路。每天早上我们得开汽车去上课。

6. 冬天相当冷，而且常下雪，我们的汽车常常停在路上坏了。

7. 老何在后头用力推，小张在前头用力拉。

8. 我们都想换一辆 [27]新汽车，可惜我们都很穷，买不起。

9. 我们每个人，每天就吃三个鸡蛋，三天才吃一次肉。

10. 我们都喜欢吃鸡，可是鸡的价钱太贵，每只卖一块半钱。

11. 我觉得有汽车很费钱，所以主张 [28]把车卖了。可是

乡下的交通 ²⁹ 不方便，没有汽车不成。

12．后来老何出了一个主意 ³⁰，他主张我们下了课去作
　　一点儿事。

13．老何在一个旅馆里找着了事，小张在图书馆里找
　　着了事。我很懒 ³¹，所以一直 ³² 找不着事。

14．他们说我太懒，不让我吃肉。我很着急，因为我
　　最爱吃肉。

15．后来我在邮局找着了事。我每天晚上把邮局的
　　屋子收拾干净。

16．我对那个事情没有什么兴趣，并且学校的功课
　　也相当忙，所以不久我又不作事了。

17．老何说，我是一个诚实的青年 ³³，可惜太懒。

18．我说，我不是懒，我的身体不好，我得常吃肉跟
　　鸡蛋。

19．有一天我在图书馆念书，忽然接着老何打来的一
　　个电话。

20．他说：「小张忽然头痛，发烧了。刚才医生给他检
　　查了一次，说他的病很普通，可是需要吃肉跟
　　鸡。」

21．老何问我，有没有钱买鸡。我说，我连买鸡蛋的

钱都没有。

22. 我跟一个朋友借了十块钱，买了一只很重的鸡，
   一打鸡蛋，另外又买了一点儿药。

23. 我正在给小张预备饭呢，忽然来了一个警察，他
   问我，那只鸡是哪儿偷来的。

24. 我很生气的说：「我是一个诚实的青年。这只鸡是
   买来的，不是偷来的。」

25. 他说，住在我们左边儿的王先生家，昨天夜里让
   贼偷了很多东西。

26. 除了金的跟银的东西以外，那个贼另外还偷了一
   只鸡。

27. 警察走了以后，老何问我，那只鸡是不是偷来的。

28. 我用力的推了他一下 ³⁴说：「你也以为我是贼吗？」

29. 老何拉着我说：「别闹 ³⁵，别闹我是跟你开玩笑 ³⁶的。

30. 我大学毕业已经快二十年了，可是每次吃鸡的时
   候还想起我的老朋友。

第十三课　句　子

1．听说你是一个俄国留学生，你对俄国的情形一定
　　很熟吧。

2．请你告诉我，俄国政府 ²⁵ 的组织跟中国政府的一样
　　吗?

3．听说中国的人口比俄国的多好几倍，是真的吗?

4．俄国也有省，县跟市吗? 俄国的县政府跟市政府
　　的组织跟中国的一样吗?

5．我知道俄国出产铜跟铁，可是我不知道俄国也出
　　产茶叶。

6．我在北海大学学习历史跟地理，可是我对各国政
　　府的组织特别有兴趣。

7．我毕业以后计划暂时在县政府作一年事。以后或
　　是到德国去留学，或是到美国去留学。

8．我希望县政府派我到美国去参观。我现在对英文
　　很注意，天天在练习。

9．你知道不知道现在美金的市价 ²⁶ 是多少?

10．站在教堂门口 ²⁸ 的，穿深黄皮鞋的那个人，你认识

　　　吗？他是<u>上海市</u>的市长 [29]，我跟他很熟。

11. 他组织了一个春假旅行团，打算到各处去旅行。
　　　他已经请我参加了。

12. 我们计划先到<u>西湖</u>去玩儿，再到<u>广东省</u>风景好的
　　　地方去看看，最后到<u>北京</u>去参观。

13. 交通问题很容易解决，或是坐飞机，或是坐火车
　　　都成。

14. 从这儿到<u>西湖</u>去，有两条铁路，都是省政府办的。

15. 我们旅行团刚才规定，只是结婚的人可以参加，
　　　你结婚了没有？

16. 你想见见那位市长吗？我可以给你们介绍介绍。

17. 市政府后头的那所大楼就是他家。

18. 房子前头有一个大铁门，门口有草地，墙是浅红
　　　颜色的，很容易找。

19. 我们旅行团原来计划上个月到<u>西湖</u>去。

20. 可是因为我着了点儿凉，得在家里休息，所以把
　　　原来的计划改了。

21. 医生试了试我的温度，又给我照了一张 X 光象。

22. 医生叫我不要抽烟，不要讲话 [30]，并且叫护士注
　　　意我的温度。

23. 医生说，我的身体，精神都不好。他要我常到公
    园去打球。
24. 我每天或是吃一只鸡，或是吃半打鸡蛋，有的时
    候也吃肉。
25. 现在参加我们旅行团的人越来越多了，比上
    个月多了一倍。
26. 各省的人都有，有的我熟，有的我不熟。
27. 我知道<u>西湖</u>出产茶叶，除了茶叶以外我不知道还
    有什么别的出产。
28. 这次旅行各人 ³¹得自己解决吃跟住的问题。
29. 要是有的人自己不能解决，可以跟我商量，我可
    以帮他们解决。
30. 市长已经叫我注意这件事了。他要我好好儿的计
    划计划。

第十四课　句　子

1. 无论 [22] 是谁，要是他要到中国去，他得先知道一点儿中国人的风俗习惯。

2. 我有一个德国朋友，他要到中国去组织一个保险公司。

3. 可是他对中国人的风俗习惯完全 [23] 不清楚。

4. 他对中国文化，跟中国社会的经济情形也完全不知道。

5. 可是他向来喜欢跟中国人在一块儿作事。

6. 他说，中国的地方那么大，人口这么多，无论哪国都不能跟中国比较 [24]。

7. 他说，他父亲从前在中国作买卖，他卖无线电 [25]，也卖机器。

8. 无线电收音机的种类 [26] 很多；有的是美国式 [27] 的；有的是德国式的。

9. 美国式的收音机 [28] 比较重；德国式的收音机比较轻。

10. 机器的种类也很多：有的是飞机的机器，有的是汽车的机器。

11. 他父亲除了卖机器以外也卖汽油。他父亲说，那

个时候汽油的价钱很低。

12. 他父亲常常给他讲中国的故事。他父亲说，中国
    是全世界最有意思的地方。

13. 他小的时候就希望他将来能到中国去。

14. 他昨天到我家来，问了我很多关于²⁹中国的情形。

15. 他先问我中国人的风俗，习惯，后来又问我中国
    的历史跟文化。

16. 我说，中国人的风俗，习惯，跟德国人的，完全
    不一样。

17. 我又说，我对中国的文化向来很有兴趣，可是不
    敢说有研究。

18. 我们又谈了关于中国的语言，特别是文言³⁰。

19. 我说，中国各省³¹的语言都不同³²。中国的文言很难
    懂。

20. 他问我：「文言跟俗话³³一样吗？」我说，文言跟俗
    话完全不同。

21. 他又问我现在中国的经济情形。我说，我对经济
    没有什么研究。

22. 我问他，喜欢不喜欢吃中国饭。他说，他向来喜
    欢吃中国饭。

23. 中国饭的味儿香极了。将来有机会，他想学学怎么作。

24. 我问他，行李收拾好了没有。他说，一切都收拾好了。

25. 他这次坐飞机走，所以行李很轻。

26. 他把一切东西都装在一个箱子 ³⁴里。他说，那个箱子已经满了。

27. 他说，他在中国有很多朋友。他们一定会到飞机场去欢迎他。

28. 我请他给我带一点儿东西到中国去。他问我，是哪一类的东西？轻不轻？

29. 我说，是一点儿俄国出产的茶叶，我已经装在一个小盒子里了。

30. 他说：「成，无论什么都成，你交给我吧。」

第十五课 句 子

1. 一年以前我在一个空军基地作事。

2. 那个基地在中国大陆²²的北部，离太平洋就有一百公里。

3. 那个基地一共有五百架飞机，每一架飞机有一个或是两个飞行员。

4. 每一分钟有很多飞机起飞，每一分钟也有很多飞机降落²³。

5. 因为我的身体不太好，所以我不是一个飞行员。

6. 据说，飞行员很苦，每天得练习起飞跟降落。

7. 据说，要是降落的时候不小心，很危险。

8. 在基地作事的人都是中国公民²⁴。不是中国公民就不能在基地作事。

9. 据说，离我们的基地不远，有一个苏联的陆军基地。

10. 我不知道那个陆军基地有多少人。据说，比我们这儿的人多好几倍。

11. 我看见一本杂志上说，苏联现在可以动员²⁵三百万陆军。

12. 可是全世界的民主国家 ²⁶只能动员一百五十万陆军。

13. 据那本杂志说，我们政府已经请联合国 ²⁷注意这件
    事了。

14. 我们那儿各种杂志都有，可是我最喜欢看空军杂
    志。

15. 我是一个喜欢安静的人。我最怕热闹。我常常一
    个人坐在绿树底下，听鸟儿叫。

16. 有一天我正坐在树底下看杂志呢，忽然听见有人
    叫我。

17. 那个人说，刚才有一架苏联的飞机要在我们的基
    地降落。

18. 可是那架飞机飞到我们的基地以前，汽油已经用
    完了，所以掉在太平洋上了。

19. 我们已经派了两架飞机去救了。据说现在太平洋
    上的天气非常不好。

20. 我不懂，为什么我们的飞机要帮助苏联，救他们
    的飞机。

21. 后来我们的飞机回来了。我等他们降落以后，就
    跑过去问他们。

22. 他们说，他们看见那架飞机了，可是没看见飞行

员。

23. 他们的目的是去救那个飞行员，不是去救那架飞机。

24. 后来我听到无线电收音机里的消息说，那个苏联的飞行员已经让美国海军给救了。

25. 美国在日本的西部有好几个海军基地。

26. 据说，那个飞行员现在在日本西南部的一个医院里。

27. 他不愿意回苏联去。他说，回苏联去太危险，他们一定会清算 [28]他。

28. 他请美国政府帮助他，把他送到美国的西部去。

29. 他说，他要到美国去的目的，将来他可以作一个美国公民。

30. 他说，苏联空军的一切他都知道得很清楚，他可以给美国政府很多帮助。